'I joy'd when to the house of God, Go up they said to me'
(Psalm 122:1)

# 'ORDINARY PEOPLE EXTRAORDINARY GOD'

Celebrating 100 years of
God at Work
In Rosskeen Free Church

Janice Maclellan

## Christian Focus

© Rosskeen Free Church of Scotland
ISBN 185792 601 3

Published in 2000 by
Christian Focus Publications,
Geanies House, Fearn, Ross-shire,
IV20 1TW, Great Britain.

Cover design by Alister MacInnes

# Contents

Dateline of Rosskeen Parish ........................... 6

Foreword .................................................. 9

Map of Parish ........................................... 10

Preface .................................................. 11

1. Building the Church ................................. 13

2. Rev John MacDonald ................................. 17

3. Rev John R Muirden ................................. 44

4. Rev Hugh MacCallum ................................ 61

5. Rev John L MacKay .................................. 79

6. Rev Kenneth MacDonald ............................ 92

7. Rev Derek Lamont .................................. 147

8. Times Change ...................................... 182

Index .................................................. 191

# THE PARISH OF ROSSKEEN 1900 – 2000

**1902** King Edward VII and Queen Alexandra visited Invergordon (Commemorative Fountain built 1904).

**1904** Perrins family gifted Public Hall and Library to Alness. Invergordon Academy – Higher Grade Dept. opened.

**1910** Invergordon Academy – Higher Grade extension opened (now Library on High street).

**1912** Invergordon became an official Naval Base.

**1914** Outbreak of World War One. Population of Invergordon grew from 1,100 to 6,000. During the war years, it was said that 20,000 lived in immediate area.

**1915** Battle of Neuve Chapelle in France. Large numbers of Alness men killed. At the Battle of Aubers Ridge, 40 Alness and Black Isle men were killed and 60 wounded. Hogmanay: HMS Natal sunk mysteriously at anchor near Saltburn with loss of over 300 lives.

**1916** Battle of Jutland. Damaged ships came into Invergordon for repair.
'The Cottages' built by women, for dockyard workers, between Invergordon and Saltburn. They cost £100 each to build.

**1917** Refugees from Russian Revolution land at Invergordon.

**1918** End of World War One. Small holdings created at Arabella for returning servicemen: 'A land fit for heroes.'

**1919** Invergordon Dockyard closed except for fuel dept. Massive unemployment and many people left the area. Establishment of Forestry Commission helped crofting to continue.

**1924** Electricity introduced to Alness.
'La Scala' Cinema in Invergordon burned down – suspected arson.

**1926** Small holdings created at Broomhill and Tomich for returning servicemen.

**1928** Invergordon Castle demolished.

**1931** Navy Mutiny at Invergordon over pay cut – incident caused Britain to go off the Gold Standard.

**1930s** Serious outbreak of brass sickness led to increased use of machinery on farms.

Big fleets came in for exercises.

**1937** Official unemployment rate of insured persons in Ross-shire (excluding agricultural workers) was 40.6%.

Work began on underground oil tanks at Inchindown.

Evanton Aerodrome expanded.

**1938** Sunderland flying boat training base established at Alness.

Munich Crisis – Big Fleet sailed out for last time.

**1939** Outbreak of World War 2.

Three Flying Boat Squadrons stationed at Invergordon.

**1940** (June) Many local Seaforth Highlanders were part of Highland Division captured at St. Valery en Caux. They were marched to prison camp in Poland for five years, then marched 400 miles to Bavaria for liberation.

**1941** Invergordon bombed.

**1942** The county raised money to build HMS Cromarty, which sank in 1943. Money raised for a second HMS Cromarty in 1944.

Duke of Kent (youngest brother of King George VI) killed in plane crash after taking off from Alness.

**1944** Polish camp built at Alness as transit camp for Polish soldiers. German POWs at local farms e.g. Dalmore.

During World War Two Senior Invergordon Academy pupils (which included pupils from Alness) had to travel to Dingwall Academy by train (buildings being used by RAF).

**1945** End of World War Two.

**1946** Proposals for a new town of 50,000 stretching from Evanton to Rosskeen!

Forestry Commission began planting at Strathruisdale.

**1952** Invergordon Town Council met to discuss 'dying town'.

**Early** Major building of new (council) houses in Invergordon.

**1950s** Development of Hydro dams: greatly increased employment and incomes.

**1956** Naval base at Invergordon put on care and maintenance basis. Out of 170 workers, 65 lost their jobs and 65 offered employment elsewhere.

**1957** *Britannia* sailed into Firth at the head of the Home Fleet; Queen inspected the Fleet here for the last time.

**1960** Work began on construction of new Distillery at Invergordon – largest grain distillery in Europe.

Foulis, Evanton, Alness, Delny and Kildary Railway Stations closed.

**1965** Highlands and Islands Development Board formed.

**1967** Planning granted for 500 council houses in Alness.

**1968** Opening of new Invergordon Academy.

**1970** Invergordon Smelter opened. Work begins at Nigg Oil Yard (Highland Fabricators).

**1970-74** Population of Alness trebled. New council housing estates built – Westford, Milnafua, Kirkside, Firhill, Coul Park and Shillinghill, but lack of corresponding infrastructure.

**1973** Workforce at Nigg had risen from 0 to 2000 (full employment in area). Two converted cruise ships anchored at Nigg Pier to house workers.

**1974** Cromarty Firth Port Authority created.

**1976** Opening of Alness Academy.

**1979** Cromarty Bridge completed.

**1981** Smelter shut.

**1982** Local unemployment 19%

**Early 1980s** Rerouting of A9 by-passed Alness and Invergordon.

**1987** Invergordon Oil Service Base opened.

Aquascot opened in Alness

**1989** Zonal opened in Invergordon (closed 1999).

**1990** Gulf War.

**1991** Ross & Cromarty Enterprise (RACE) created.

**1993** ATC Cosmetics opened in Invergordon. Largest company of its kind in Europe.

**1997** Wind Farm built at Evanton.

**1998** B.T. Call Centre opened in Alness.

**1980/ 1990s** Fluctuating employment at Nigg and Ardersier oil yards continues historical cycle of boom and poverty.

# FOREWORD

Rosskeen Free Church this year (2000) celebrates a centenary of worshipping God in our present building.

This book attempts to document something of 100 years of God at work in the lives of ordinary people. The early chapters give a glimpse into church and home life in the early part of this century, and the faithful and prayerful preaching of the Word of God over time. The seeds of that Word and prayer bear their fruit in the latter decades, when there is a good deal of growth in Rosskeen. The later chapters of the book attempt to describe something of the excitement of this time, through stories of how Jesus Christ came into lives and changed them forever, by having their sins forgiven and coming to know the peace and joy of God.

We trust and pray that there is much fruit yet to come, and that the walls of Rosskeen Church will one day be unable to contain the congregation as we gather to praise and worship our great and glorious Lord.

'I kneel before the Father, from whom the whole family in heaven and on earth derives its name. I pray that out of his glorious riches he may strengthen you with power through his Spirit in your inner being, so that Christ may dwell in your hearts through faith. And I pray that you, being rooted and established in love, may have power, together with all the saints, to grasp how wide and long and high and deep is the love of Christ, and to know this love that surpasses knowledge – that you may be filled to the measure of all the fulness of God.

'Now to him who is able to do immeasurably more than all we ask or imagine, according to his power that is at work within us, to him be glory in the church and in Christ Jesus throughout all generations, for ever and ever! Amen' (Eph. 3:14-21).

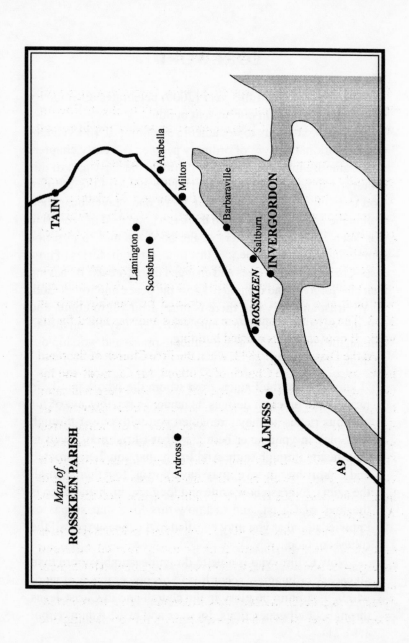

*Map of*
**ROSSKEEN PARISH**

TAIN

Arabella
Milton

Lamington
Scotsburn

Barbaraville

Saltburn
*ROSSKEEN*
INVERGORDON

Ardross

ALNESS

A9

# PREFACE

Although this book is concerned with God's dealings with Rosskeen Free Church from 1900 to 2000, the following information may be of some interest in setting the historical context.

David Carment, who was born in Keiss, Caithness, in 1772, originally came to Rosskeen as parish minister on 14th March, 1822 (i.e. he was the Church of Scotland Minister). The congregation at that time worshipped in a building within the cemetery grounds at Lower Rosskeen, part of the ruins of which may still be seen there.

The church building standing in the cemetery at present was built during Mr Carment's ministry. It seated 1360 people, and was built at a cost of £2,027. It opened for worship early in 1833. The architect came from Inverness and was noted for his work. It now stands as a listed building.

At the Disruption of 1843, when the Free Church of Scotland broke away from the Church of Scotland, Mr Carment and his congregation, all but one family, left lower Rosskeen and came to Achnagarron to choose a site to build a new church. The foundation stone of the original Free Church at Achnagarron was laid in the summer of 1844 by General Munro of Teaninich. On 20th April 1845, this church was opened for worship by Dr Gustavus Aird, Creich, and Mr Carment. This church, built to hold 1400, was thus the first building on the present site at Achnagarron, Rosskeen.

In fact, during Rev David Carment's time in Rosskeen, three churches were built and four schools opened between Invergordon and Saltburn, with his encouragement. Mr Carment knew much personal sorrow in his life, with most of his family dying young. In the midst of this, in January 1841, he reported: 'There has been since 1840 a very remarkable awakening and religious revival in this parish and neighbourhood, especially among the young; and numbers I have reason to believe, have been savingly converted.'[1]

Rev John Hutcheson Fraser was called as colleague and successor to David Carment in 1853, and on 26th May 1856, in his 84th year, Mr Carment died. In 1861, a separate charge of Invergordon was formed, and a church was built in Invergordon, which is now the Church of Scotland. Mr Fraser died in January 1884.

In 1885, the Rev John Ross was ordained at Rosskeen, and he remained there until 1900, when he joined the United Free Church. Mr Ross died on June 2nd 1934, in his 81st year.

The congregation was without a minister from the time of Rev Ross's departure until 1908.

---

1. H Sprange, *Kingdom Kids*, Christian Focus Publications, p.85

# CHAPTER 1

## BUILDING THE CHURCH

The Building Committee of Rosskeen Free Church met on 6 July 1898, in the Free Church Hall, Bridgend, Alness, with Mr John Ross, Seaforth, in the chair. It was decided to build a new Free Church at Achnagarron, which is the present church building and the second one on that site. Present at the meeting were: Major MacKenzie, Messrs John Reid, Coliemore; Hugh Ferguson, Achnagarron; David Ross; and John MacKenzie, precentor. Mr James Maitland, Architect, Tain was there with the offers from several contractors.

The successful contractors and their prices were:

| Wm Ross, Tain | Mason | £1760: 0:0 |
|---|---|---|
| Nicol & Son, Tain | Carpenters | 875: 0:0 |
| Wm Urquhart, Tain | Painter | 130: 0:0 |
| MacDonald Ross, Tain | Slater | 99: 0:0 |
| MacRae & Sons, Tain | Plumbers | 43:15:0 |
| Rose St. Foundry, Inverness | Iron | 65: 0:0 |
| Rose St. Foundry, Inverness | Heating | 62: 0:0 |
| John Munro, Tain | Plasterer | 183:10:0 |
| | | £3218: 5:0 |

The building, to seat 1,000, when approached from Rosskeen Bridge, has a strange two-dimensional appearance, which is very unusual.

Most of the total cost of the building came from a bequest by the Denoon family, to whom a marble memorial stone is in the vestibule. The Denoon family gave generously to the cause of the Church of Christ in Invergordon and Rosskeen, both in years of service and money.

They lived in Auchentoul and had a grain merchant's business

in Invergordon. Mr Denoon, an elder in the congregation for
some fifty years, and treasurer of the Sustentation Fund for most
of that time, must have come into the Free Church at the
Disruption. Mr Denoon and his sister gave generously to the
Free Church both at Rosskeen and Invergordon, and money left
to Rosskeen at their deaths was used in the building of the present
church.

Growing up at the smiddy next door to the church, Mr A G
MacKenzie has stories of the building in progress: 'Today's
Rosskeen Free Church is built inside the foundations of the
original church. If you look in through the lower vents of the
outside walls of the church today (best done at dusk with a good
torch) you will see the rubble left by the builders, and the stones
on which the floor beams are resting.

'I know that four workmen were sacked during the building
of the church. One was sacked for knocking off what looks like
a lion's head on top of the pillars at the front door. Another was
sacked, also for carelessness while carrying a plank. The third, a
joiner, spoiled the frame on the east stair. The mistake can be
seen in the cupboard under the stairs. I do not know what
happened to the fourth man. I know these details because my
grandmother lodged several of the workmen in her house down
at the smiddy.

'In the field to the west of the church there was a shed called
the "hewing shed". Here the stones that built the church were
dressed and shaped. Between 5th December 1898 and 17th
August 1899, 38,379 tools were sharpened. These tools were
chisels, cloorers and jumpers, all for dressing stone. The
sharpening was done in the smithy fire. I have taken these figures
from the daybook at Achnagarron Smithy. There was no mention
of price.'

The wood used to build the church is pitch pine. It came from
Russia, and was landed at Belleport, the small jetty below
Rosskeen, probably by coasters via a major port. At that time,
much of the building timber was coming in from Russia and

will be found in many local houses built around then. Kenny and Reta MacDonald's new home, the old manse at Resolis, is beautifully finished with the same wood, and they were recently told that to buy even a little of such wood nowadays would cost a small fortune.

This particular type of wood is apparently immune to woodworm, and so ideal for building a church. It has indeed stood the test of time – the interior of Rosskeen today is immaculate, with the glowing warmth and beauty of the colours and textures of the pine.

A.G.'s grandmother and Jessie Reid used to recall the services being held in the wood on the right hand side of the road, opposite Mr Nigel Ross's house, about 500 yards from the church, while the new church was being built.

His late father used to say that in the years after the new church was opened, you had to be in church very early on a Communion Sunday or you would not get a seat. The late Mrs Beana MacBean used to recall that when she was a young girl, the church was full upstairs and downstairs, with three front rows reserved for elderly people with hearing problems, as there were no hearing aids in those days.

14th June 1900 was the Fast Day preceding the Communion Sabbath and, as now, was on a Thursday. That day, the new Free Church at Rosskeen was opened for public worship. The worship started with Rev Murdo MacKenzie, Free North Church, Inverness, preaching. The service began at 11.30am, all in Gaelic, with the text: Matthew 16:18: 'And I say also unto thee, that thou art Peter and upon this rock I will build my church; and the gates of hell shall not prevail against it.' At 1.30pm, Rev I. I. Black, LLD, preached in English from Hebrews 9:14: 'How much more shall the blood of Christ, who through the eternal spirit offered himself without spot to God, purge your conscience from dead works to serve the living God.' The evening service was taken by Rev John Noble, Lairg, preaching in English from Daniel.

The Sabbath Communion Service was conducted by Rev Archibald Beaton, Free Church of Urray, preaching on 1 Peter 2:9: 'But ye are a chosen generation, a royal priesthood, a holy nation, a peculiar people; that ye should show forth the praises of him who hath called you out of darkness into his wonderful light' (AV).

# CHAPTER 2

# REV JOHN MACDONALD

Rev John MacDonald became minister of Rosskeen in 1908.

We asked some of the people who have been longest associated with our church to share their earliest memories with us. Taken together, they provide us with a glimpse of church-life in the early part of this century.

The contributors are:

| | |
|---|---|
| Mrs Mary Dryden (nee MacKay) | (MD) |
| Mrs Joan MacIntosh | (JMI) |
| Mrs Ena MacIver | (EM) |
| Mrs Jean MacKay | (JM) |
| Mr A G MacKenzie | (AGM) |
| Mr David MacLeod | (DM) |
| Mr Walter MacLeod | (WM) |
| Mrs Mary Manson (nee Aird) | (MM) |
| Mrs Jenny Peterkin (nee Winchester) | (JP) |
| Mrs Dolly Mackenzie | (DMK) |

**The MacDonalds**

Mrs Mary Dryden was born in 1908 – in the same year as Rev John MacDonald and his family came to Rosskeen: 'Mr MacDonald was the minister when I first went to church in Rosskeen. He and his wife had a big family: John, Alasdair, Mary, Cathy, Isa, Jeannie and Ada. I went to Sunday School with Isa. My recollection of Mrs MacDonald is of a very kind lady and my recollection of Mr MacDonald is of him being very strict. I remember somebody going dancing and getting a good telling-off. Ministers nowadays are definitely less formal.'

Mr Walter MacLeod (who sadly died on 16th October, 1999) recalled: 'Rev John MacDonald was very strict about behaviour in God's house, and everything was done in a very orderly

17

fashion; if there was the slightest noise from the Sunday School he would knock on the partition saying: "Quiet, children, please!" Ministers always wore their collar, and he would be dressed the same for home visits.'

The late Mrs Jean MacKay, who was born in 1908 and sadly passed away on 12 April 1998, used to go to the manse in her teens to work, doing washing and other household chores: 'When Rev MacDonald paid a visit to the house, the youngsters had to sit very quietly while the adults conversed. Present day ministers differ from those in my youth in that they are much more approachable these days, but both Mr and Mrs MacDonald were always very nice.'

Mrs Joan MacIntosh lives in Inverness, and worships at the Free North Church: 'I can't tell you much about his preaching – at first I was too young to "take it in". He was a very clever man and I think that probably his preaching was above my understanding. What I can say is that he was a very "real" minister. He was one of the nicest and most genuine of men I have ever known. He didn't look a strong man, but I can't remember him ever being ill.

'He was constantly at the bedside of those who were ill and my own mother was greatly comforted by his many visits over the long years of her illness. He, himself, and Mrs MacDonald, knew much sorrow over the loss of a young son and beautiful daughter – but it is not for me to encroach on their grief.'

Mr MacDonald came to church in his pony and trap. One pony was 'skittish' and eventually, while travelling to a service in Ardross, the pony bolted and he was thrown from the trap, dislocating his shoulder. Some time later he got his first car!

In 1908, work was carried out on the manse:

### MANSE RENOVATION BILL

| | | |
|---|---|---|
| Mason work (concrete) | W & J Tuach | £ 29: 0: 0 |
| Plumber work | Wm Tolmie | 30: 7: 6 |
| Carpenter work | Mr A Minto | 30:15: 8 |
| Iron work | A MacKenzie & Son | 3: 0: 0 |
| Heating Apparatus | A MacKenzie & Son | 5:10: 0 |
| Mason work | W & J Tuach | 3:17: 0 |
| | | 102:10: 2 |

**Family life**

Mrs Joan MacIntosh, who was born in 1905, gives a glimpse into her family home: 'My mother's father was a ploughman in Ardross. He was known as one of "The Men". He and my grandmother were Gaelic speakers, having originally come from the Ullapool area. They had a family of four sons and four daughters. My grandfather taught his family Gaelic by reading a Gaelic Bible "round the table". At least one of my aunts wasn't very good at it and my mother was often in trouble for laughing at her. It was quite common for my grandfather, Alex Cameron, to walk to Dingwall and back to hear a preacher named Dr Kennedy (and he would not be the only one going). The sons got an Academy education by walking the back road to Tain every Monday morning and home on Friday evening. Only one, John, went to University – they were too poor to send the others. The four girls went "into service" after primary school in Ardross. My Uncle John became a Free Church Minister – Prof. John Kennedy Cameron. My mother's closeness to him had a bearing on my own name.'

Mrs Dolly MacKenzie writes: 'In the latter part of this century change has occurred at a speed never seen before. In the earlier part of the century a strict Presbyterian upbringing was fairly widespread, and something very different from its counterpart nowadays. There was not the same crisis of authority. At home, parents were very much in charge whether that authority was used "wisely or too well".

'In the Sutherland congregation where my own childhood was spent, family worship was the norm in every household. Bibles in Gaelic and English, religious biographies and collections of sermons exceeded any other books in number in our house. These Bibles were opened three times a day for worship, or "taking the books" as it was called. The Old Testament was the morning reading and the New Testament was read at bedtime. A psalm was read each time and part of it was sung, using the "putting out the line" method of precenting, and prayer finished the worship. At mid day there was more psalm singing and an extra worship was always taken when anyone was leaving home. It made this emotionally charged time longer, but the hope always was for the travellers to have "journeying mercies".

'At home, we youngsters had to undergo many lively question and answer sessions, taken by the adults in the household and relating to what had been read in the Bible. A quiz might start up at any time with questions like, "What does Ebenezer mean?" or "Where does Rahab fit into David's family tree?" The grounding we were given in the text of the Authorised Version was extremely thorough. Even a small mistake in a quotation was treated as a "clanger".

'Then there was the Shorter Catechism. By the time we had finished primary school we were expected to be word perfect from number 1 to number 107. On a Sabbath afternoon when the weather was too stormy for church, or if adults were well enough rested, a catechising session was held. Father had the catechism and everyone present was expected to answer the questions through the whole range, question about. I don't recollect much sticking but I know that today I would need a hint or two about how to start the answers to the "required" and "forbidden" in the Commandments.

'During our childhood, we youngsters were very much seen and not heard. Up until the age of seven we had to stand for meals. These meals always began and ended with grace.

'Home, church and school worked hand in glove regarding our religious education. At school the teachers took "Bible" really seriously. At primary level "Bible" was the first lesson each day. Often in winter our mouths would be stiff from cold after a long walk over the moor, but we still had to recite the set piece from chapter, psalm or catechism! By the time we had reached third year secondary we had learned the whole of the Sermon on the Mount, as told in Matthew chapters 5, 6 and 7, and we'd also learned many other chapters, texts and psalms.

'From fourth year onwards, "Bible" was taken by Mr Sam Will, later a missionary in Peru. We didn't have to learn anything by heart, but Mr Will chose the topics and led many productive discussions. The oral Bible exam was in June, for the whole school. Other lessons were suspended and a period of intense revision entered into. All the local ministers advanced on the school on a set day. The teachers feared getting our Free Presbyterian minister as he was a very strict questioner! Usually, children from his own congregation were placed along the front of the class.

'However, he avoided questioning them as he knew what they could do. While we got off nearly scot free children from the other churches took the brunt of the questioning. Youngsters who left home to work or study were given a Bible. On the fly leaf of mine the minister wrote the verse I was to keep before me, Psalm 9, verse 10.

'Perhaps the memories most deeply etched on my mind from childhood are the "church" memories. "Sunday trading", even the word would have been an anathema, was unthinkable. The services held on the Sabbath were in Gaelic at 12, English at 1, then Sunday School at 5 and the English evening service at 6. We had to attend them all, although only the adults in the household spoke Gaelic. The English services were very long, a minimum of one and a half hours, at times even an hour and forty minutes. Only works of necessity were attempted in the home on the Sabbath. Even the dishes were not washed but piled up for what must have been a punishing Monday morning. On Saturday, food that could be prepared and cooked was made ready to be set out for meals the following day. All the footwear for churchgoers had to be polished up. We did have cold water in the house but it wasn't drinkable, so extra pails of water were drawn from the well. No one approached a well on Sabbath! The animals on the croft did not occasion Sunday work either! One Saturday chore we children had was to sit like little elves on the barn floor and hammer sheets of oil-cake into small pieces. Often, we had to

carry in part of a corn stack to be put through the threshing mill
on the Saturday. This process produced a great deal of dust in
the barn, but, fortunately, none of us succumbed to farmer's lung!

'The Communion season was again somewhat different from
today. Our parish had only one communion, on the first Sabbath
in July. The school always closed the day before the Fast Day,
as indeed it closed for the Harvest Thanksgiving. Church people
came from places like Raasay, Harris, Strathy, Lochinver,
Scourie, Kinlochbervie, Halkirk, not forgetting Rogart and
Creich. These visitors stayed with church families for the
duration, and a minority moved from one communion to the
next from June to September, so they must have been away from
home a good while. There were always two visiting ministers.
On the Thursday there were ordinary Gaelic and English services.
Friday was the "men's day" when the male members "spoke to
the question", which meant expounding a text chosen by a
minister, who himself gave the last word on that subject. There
was an ordinary service on Friday evening, and again Gaelic
and English services on Saturday. No service was held on
Saturday evening so as to give those in the congregation taking
part in the communion, time to "be still". Every morning at 8am
there was a prayer meeting. The action service on Sunday always
lasted four hours. The English service was in the school and
Gaelic in the church and there was a half mile walk between
them. All the congregation was present in the church for the
English table, the Gaelic table having already been served.
Sunday evening thanksgiving service was in English. The church
was usually crowded then, as there was no service in Creich or
Rogart. Monday's service was held early, as people from
Lochinver, Scourie and Kinlochbervie had to have a meal before
catching the bus back home.

'Monday's service was devoted to advising "our young
people". I clearly recall that advice. Inevitably there was a sense
of loneliness after the stir of the communion. I remember
Professor MacIntosh preaching on that very theme on a Monday

evening service in our church here. He spoke of when Mary and Joseph couldn't find Jesus on their way home. "How," he asked, "did they solve their problem and end their perplexity?" "They went back to Jesus," was his answer.'

## Sunday School

Joan MacIntosh believes that 'one of the directions in which the aspect of the church has changed, and rightly so, is in their attitude to children. Yes, I went to Sunday School – our two teachers being my father and Mr Urquhart, the shoemaker. And they were very nice. Then they stopped and we had to go to the church that bit earlier. I remember that Mrs MacDonald was my teacher there, and there were some other lady teachers. It was that way when I left.

'Sometime during these years we had to learn the whole Catechism. We had to go to the schoolmaster to repeat the questions. I went along with my sister, Bessie. She did well and got a Bible as a prize – but I soon got stuck. I seem to have a memory for all the wrong things!! It's a joy today to see how the little ones are catered for. Thinking back, I think that Mr and Mrs MacDonald realised that children were not treated as real feeling people, because they held parties for them at special times.

'Each summer we had a Sunday School picnic, which was well attended by young and old. It was always in a field some miles from home. I can't remember how we got there, but it always seemed to be a good dry day. We always enjoyed those picnics. There was plenty to eat, we all got "baggies", and there were lots of races. The races were rather a sore point with me. I was very thin – all arms and legs, and everyone expected me to win, but I knew how stiff my knees were. I could not run very fast – so I always came in last. I didn't mind that in itself, but it was such a personal disgrace when so much was expected of me.

'I could sometimes redeem myself in the "egg and spoon", the "three-legged" and the "bag race", as they didn't depend on speed.'

Down at the church, Mr MacDonald set up the Sunday School to run in the two vestries at 11am, while the Gaelic service went on in the church.

Mrs Jenny Peterkin was born in 1913 and has been part of Rosskeen Congregation since she was four years old. She remembers the Sunday School classes – two classes in the top vestry, and two classes in the bottom vestry (which must have been a bit of a squeeze!) Her teachers were Mrs Ross, Miss Munro, Miss Bell and Miss Munro.

'Welfare of Youth Examinations (Sunday School Exams) were held in the old manse. Candidates would sit and do half of the examination and then they would go out and search for "hidden treasures" in the bushes, before doing the second half of the paper. Mrs MacDonald always provided children with a beautiful tea and home baking. It was a great day!

'The children sat around the big dining-room table. Mrs MacDonald, the minister's wife, would walk around the table, keeping a watchful eye on the children as they wrote out their answers.'

Mrs Ena MacIver, who still lives in the Alness house she was born in, also remembers following the Welfare of Youth syllabus, and the exams in the manse. Her teachers were Mrs MacDonald, the minister's wife, Miss Helen Munro, Miss Katie Munro and Miss Stewart. She remembers being asked to learn 'off by heart' a verse of a psalm, catechism and a portion of scripture.

Mrs Mary Manson's parents attended Rosskeen Church regularly and she was baptised there in 1929 – the year she was born. Her parents took her to church at the age of two years. She started attending Sunday School at the age of five years, which was held from 11am until 11.45am. Her father took her on the bar of his bike. She remembers two teachers, 'Mr and Mrs MacDonald's daughter, Isa, and Miss Stewart, who also taught in Alness primary school and lodged with Miss Helen Munro, who had the Draper's Shop. Sunday School was held in the vestry rooms at the back of the church which was heated by coal fires. The attendance was small – about twenty maybe. Rev Alastair Ross was a pupil while I was there.

'We were taught stories of Jesus; we memorised verses from chapters in the Bible and learned quite a lot of the psalms. Sometimes we got nice little cards with a text on them.

'After Sunday School, I stayed for the English service at 12 noon.

'A picnic was held each year, usually locally – Ardross, Evanton and Alness being some of the places I remember.

'At New Year time we all went to the manse for a special tea. My early years in church were during the Second World War. The congregation was so small that the morning service was held in the vestry rooms during the winter.'

Mr A G MacKenzie of the Smiddy, Achnagarron, remembers a proud moment of his childhood. 'Away back in 1935, one of the teachers who taught the younger children was Miss Isa MacDonald, the minister's daughter. Then came a Miss Stewart from Kyle. She taught in the day-school in Alness West School (not Bridgend). Houses now stand where the school was. It was commandeered by the Army when the war begun. The Headmaster retired and Miss Stewart moved to Bridgend School.

'Isa MacDonald was by now engaged to the Rev Donald MacKay, Watten. My father and mother used to visit Mr and Mrs D W Ross, Glasgow House, Alness, every Saturday evening. (They were the parents of Rev Alastair Ross, ex-Strathpeffer, Glasgow, Oban and Edinburgh). There my parents heard that the powers-that-were in the church were giving Miss MacDonald a presentation, jointly from the congregation and the Sunday School. I had been picked to make the Sunday School presentation. At home, I was well drilled in saluting, something you hardly ever see a youngster doing to a teacher nowadays. The presentation was to be made in the policies of Ardross Castle, where the annual picnic was going to take place. (Mr Dyson Perrins generously allowed the use of the Castle Grounds for social purposes to those congregations who worshipped in Ardross Church until 1937, when he sold out).

'It must have been the estate workers who fixed swings to the branches of the trees at the castle. They made a secure job of this. I remember having a good swing and thoroughly enjoying myself, when the call came: "The Presentation!" I was dragged away to do it, and still have a large photograph of the occasion.'

## Going to church

*Mr Davie MacLeod*
'I remember well the lovely walk from Millcraig to the Sabbath School each Sunday. The hand of God was to be seen all around: in the variety of wild flowers; in the birds nesting in grassy banks, dykes, whins and broom; and in the farm stock grazing nearby, especially in the sight of a mare and her foal.

'Sometimes it happened that we met Mr Donald Ross, Stoney-field, at the crossroads below Culcairn, and got a lift – pony and trap was the transport. Mr Ross was a lovely man, and a solid elder in Rosskeen for many years, as was his father before him.

'The stables were situated at the west side of the church, by the steeple. One could hold four or five ponies, and the other was bigger still. When we got to the church, Mr Ross would show us how to unyoke the pony and fold the harness. Apart from those who had a pony and trap, everyone walked to church. Now and then we would see the odd bike.

'Before the 1920s, families walked from Dalnevie and Stittenham to both services on Sundays. Returning home from the morning service, they had just time for a quick cup of tea before they set off again for the evening service.

'The little field adjacent to the church used to have a stable for coach horses. The field became overgrown with broom. Tinkers passing the road used to camp in the field and sometimes there were fights among them. Meantime, horse numbers were declining, and cars and bicycles were increasing. It was decided to take down the original stable and build one at the top of the field for just six horses. This stable was taken down about 1947, when John Ross, Seaforth House, was Session Clerk. He got these stables to use as a garden shed.

'Inside the Church, up in the gallery, the corner seats were reserved for coachmen. They had to get out before the service ended, to get the horses harnessed and yoked into the coaches.'

At about five years of age, Mrs Jean MacKay used to walk from her home at Millcraig to the church and Sunday School. Her grandparents used to walk from Stittenham. She remembers one Sunday when she had been sitting up in the gallery with her granny, she felt that she ought to go home with her granny, because she didn't want her to go home on her own. Whilst walking along the road near Nonikiln, they met a sailor who looked very suspicious. He had his hat pulled down far over his face and his collar well up too, so that all they could see were his eyes. Jean felt so thankful that she had been there to accompany her granny – even though she was only about seven years old!

Both Mrs Mary Manson and Mrs Ena MacIver remember being taken to church on the bar of their father's bike. Mary's father, John Aird, used to cycle up about 10.45am for the Gaelic Service and then wait on for the English at 12 o' clock.

Mrs MacIver sometimes got home in the pony and trap belonging to Mr Urquhart, the shoemaker. She remembers Mrs Ross, who at 92 years old, would walk from Invergordon to the church, and no adverse weather would stop her.

Mr Walter MacLeod recalled the walk to Rosskeen, dressed in their 'Sunday Best'. In the summertime they would be barefoot. Because of the distance, the young ones didn't go to the evening service, but his father would cycle to it. People walked regardless of the weather conditions.

Mrs Mary Dryden agrees: 'The weather didn't play any part in whether you went to church or not. Rain, hail or shine – ALWAYS! Women took the children with them wherever they went.'

Mrs Joan MacIntosh became slowly conscious that she

belonged to the Free Church as she grew up. 'Initially, a vague
feeling of being the one and "only true church among churches"
continued to colour our lives for many years. In those days there
were big families, and as children grew up and made their own
friends the tension slowly grew less, and bridges were steadily
built with those neighbouring churches which also preach the
gospel of Jesus Christ crucified.

'Rosskeen Church is 1.5 miles from the village (Alness).
Some people came from Ardross, some from Invergordon, and
some from farms and crofts around and east of the church. I
don't remember my first time of going there – just the Sunday
walk, with my father always there, and often my mother too,
and then the rest of us.

'After about half a mile we would pass my auntie's croft,
and then on between the two woods – a dark one with big trees
on the left (that was where we got blaeberries), and a brighter
wood with smaller, deciduous trees on the right hand side. That
was where we got our tadpoles in a wee pond, and often found
bird's nests. We kept the eggs in long boxes with four or five
divisions and a glass top. We got the boxes from the draper's
shop when the stock of men's ties was finished. Before reaching
the end of the woods, we came to the mile-stone – always crooked
in the ground.

'Soon we were in open space on either side, with a few houses
and crofts on the left and big cultivated fields to the right. Then
came the burn and we always had to say "Hullo" to the fish, and
then it was time to enter the church, but not before having a look
over at the stables to note whose horses and machines were there.
We never strayed over, so I don't know exactly how many there
were, but I should think about two dozen. At that time, there
were no cars.

'The main road was in front of the church, and there was a
raised bank, which in summer was blue with cuckoo flowers – I
can see them now. All-in-all, it was a lovely walk on a summer's
day – not only for us, but for many families from the village.

'On entering the church, we duly put our pennies (and pennies it was) in the plate. These had been issued to us before leaving home.

'Now let's suppose we're going home from church. There were a very few machines. One belonged to Mr and Mrs McLennan, Moultivie. They gave lifts to as many as possible. Mostly, I refused. This was because my father was later than the others – he stayed behind to count the pennies, which he then carried home. They were kept in a locked drawer until it was time to send them to the bank. When I was older, I would wait for him, as I was sorry for him having to come home alone. He never grumbled about the weight of the pennies. I just wondered if he would be feeling a wee bit tired. Then, at a particular point on the road, he would suddenly mention a few names and say: "Why don't they come to church? Sleeping! Sleeping all day! Sleeping themselves into train-oil!" At this he would give a kind of snort. I often wanted to ask him what was different about train-oil, but I never dared, especially after he gave the snort. To this day, I don't know what train-oil is.

'Before I became my father's "keeper", I used to walk home like the others – family-wise. There we were, in threes and fours and twos. There was a young woman who was wearing a widow's "fall". I liked walking behind her. The "fall" was of soft grey stuff and fell in such lovely smooth pleats – it was so neat. So long ago!

'On at least one occasion I came home with another girl – Minnie – the schoolmaster's daughter. She was a year older than me, and we still write and see each other occasionally. This day we were in sombre mood. We were nearing home when we were discussing "Hell-Fire". Quite seriously, I asked Minnie how big it would be, suggesting the width of a certain field. Minnie considered. A few yards further on there was a small gate. Minnie thought my estimation was on the small side, but if you took it to that wee gate, that should be about right! I, of course, bowed to the superior knowledge of the schoolmaster's daughter. The discussion had been quite serious!

'Thinking back, there was little of the friendliness of friends that we really were. In this, again there is a change for the better.

'One of the first to have a car was the Rev Alastair Ross' father – a Morris Cowley. Soon there were others, and they were very generous with lifts. The atmosphere was changing.'

## Rev Alastair Ross' story

'Rosskeen was my church until I was called up in 1942, and the Rev John MacDonald was my first minister.

'Going to church was for me an utter bore and, due to that, my behaviour apparently left very much to be desired. But during the closing years of Mr MacDonald's ministry this attitude began to wear off and I actually came to enjoy the experience. In my simplicity (to say nothing of my ignorance) I thought it was all because the minister's preaching had "improved"! The truth was that the improvement was in me as a result of the preaching, for I had begun to listen for the first time.

'I cannot remember anything in particular Mr MacDonald said, but I do recall something particular he regularly did – and that was visiting. He was an assiduous pastor who had a genuine concern for his flock. Sometimes he would walk from the manse at Rosskeen to Alness in order to visit. I heard my parents say how much his visiting was appreciated not only by his own people but by others on whom he called when they were in trouble.

'This wider concern for the community was also evidenced when, for example, he joined with local Church of Scotland ministers in a service of "humiliation and prayer" held in the Alness Town Hall during the war. This, let it be said, was no easy thing for a deeply committed Free Church minister to do in those days.

'My continuing interest in Rosskeen, therefore, was due in no small way to the fact that my first interest in the gospel was kindled there. On returning from the RAF and having applied for the Free Church ministry, it was Mr MacDonald who supported my application at the Presbytery, perhaps a year or so before he retired.

'So this little story is about a man whose faithful ministry encouraged at least one lad from Rosskeen to seek the road that leads us to the Lamb. It's only when we behold and bow before that Lamb in the submission of faith that we can call ourselves Christians and can rejoice in hope of the glory of God. May many more in Rosskeen have this hope.'

## Sabbaths

'We never said "Sunday", it was always "Sabbath.' (JMI).

'Our Sabbaths were spent very quietly. We would walk to Rosskeen – first we went to Sabbath School and while that was on the Gaelic Service would be held. We then went to the English Service. We never visited people's homes on a Sunday, like we do today – they were strictly family days.' (WM)

'In the afternoon we visited my grandparents, who lived about a mile away. I had to sit very quiet and still while they talked. We returned home in time for the evening service, in the Hall at Perrins Road. Sunday was very much a "day of rest" and prayers.' (MM)

'Sabbaths were very strict – we weren't allowed out even for a walk. My dad examined everything I read – if it wasn't "The Christian Herald" – oh dear! I was eventually allowed out for a walk, but I can't remember when that was. Saturday evening was spent preparing everything for the following day.' (MD)

'Sunday afternoons were mostly spent indoors, where I along with other members of my family sang psalms and hymns. On occasion, my mother would take the family for a walk along the side of a field through the woods. I was never allowed to go out and play.' (JM)

'Lessons for Sunday School were prepared before Church. Psalms were sung using a modulator on the wall. Absolutely no cooking was done on a Sunday – everything was prepared on the Saturday. Meat would be heated up in the soup. Books were read in the afternoon – it was a "Family Day".' (EM)

## Dress

'In my day, no-one ever came disrespectfully dressed, no matter how poor a family was. No woman ever came without a hat and men never wore casual dress. Ministers were always dressed with their "collars" and they would be dressed the same for home visits.' (WM)

'Everybody was dressed in their "best clothes", which were only worn for church.' (MM)

'Proper Sunday clothes were always worn, regardless of being poor or well off.' (JP)

Mrs Jean MacKay remembered her special Sunday clothes – a nice little straw hat with flowers on it, and elasticated under the chin. Jean had always worn a hat to church and would have found it hard not to wear one. Shoes were worn on Sundays and also during the week in colder months, but Jean hated wearing footwear. Jean inherited her cousin Alec's old boots when he got new ones. When they got home from church her good clothes were all put away and she had to put on her old clothes.

'I remember my father in his tile hat and a sort of black frock coat, which he wore on Communion Sundays and also at funerals. This fashion of dress must have died out fairly early on.' (JMI)

'Clothes were long and black. Widows never wore anything but black. I wore my "Sunday Best" – which was not worn any other day except special occasions, e.g. my Dad and Step-mother's wedding.' (EM)

## Special occasions

'In days gone by, Fast Days and Harvest Thanksgiving Days were school and shop holidays. The winter Fast Day was the first Thursday in November, and the Harvest Thanksgiving was the third Thursday in November.

'In the first half of this century, a man who wanted baptism for his infant used to have to apply to the minister and to answer questions as to what he believed and to recite answers to the Shorter Catechism questions. Nerves made the latter an ordeal for some, but the catechism was much better known then than it is today. In those days, only the man made the baptismal vows. Few baptisms were in the church – most were at home. Families were big and there were no crèches to put other children into. There was little or no family transport. One old lady told me that her cousin, oldest of a family of eight, went to his baptism in a cart pulled by a horse, on a very wet Sabbath, when the baby was only weeks old. That baptism was in church.

'Funerals used to go mainly from the house where the deceased used to live. Only in the last thirty-odd years did church funerals come in.

'Church marriages were rare too, as there was no heating or lighting in the church. People were married in hotels, or, if there was good reason such as a family bereavement etc., the marriage was conducted in the manse. Farm workers used to get a few hours off work to get married, and then went back to attend to the animals in the evening.' (AGM)

Mrs Ena MacIver and her husband Kenny were married in the Station Hotel by Rev John MacDonald from Kiltearn, because Mrs MacDonald, the wife of Rev John MacDonald, Rosskeen, had died that week. No weddings or funerals were held in the church at that time. Her daughter Mhairi's wedding in 1966 was the first she remembers attending in Rosskeen.

Mrs Jean MacKay and her husband were married in the Free Church Hall in Perrins Road, Alness in 1926.

Jean's mother looked after the Hall, and Jean would lend a hand there too.

Jean also remembers that Christmas wasn't kept, but New Year was. Every New Year, Jean got a new ribbon, which she loved to show off to visitors on New Year's Day.

### Church services
'Rosskeen Church is beautiful, inside and out. I think there are extensions to it now, but there were none in my day. It was heated in winter by a furnace, and Mr MacKenzie, Achnagarron, was

responsible for that. The seating is pretty much as it is in most old churches, with the main seating part in the middle and two side seating parts. The gallery, as in many churches, was not used. Now I look back and I see many of the churchgoers I used to know.

'In front of the pulpit was the elders' box, and the precentors sat facing the congregation. To the minister's left, and at right angles to the congregation, sat his own family, and Mr John Reid's family also shared these side seats. To the minister's right, on the opposite side, sat the Ross family and my Auntie Charlotte and family. Mr Donald Ross, Stoneyfield, and his family sat down at the front, and behind them were the "Handers" family, and behind them sat the Ross family, Glasgow House. Miss Munro, the draper sat on the left hand part, and at the back were Mr and Mrs Urquhart and their son Hughie, and Mr MacKay, the schoolmaster and his family.' (JMI)

Comparing the early part of this century with today, near the end, what are the main differences that people can see?

'The order of the service is much the same, the only difference, I think, is that our sermons and prayers were much longer then. We also only had two communions (instead of four as now), in June and November, from Thursdays to Mondays. The Thursdays were school and shop holidays. There were no extra services and meetings like today, apart from the Prayer Meeting.' (WM)

'The number of meetings has increased, especially for the women and for the young people.' (MM)

'The difference between then and now is the number of people coming. It was such a small congregation then.' (MD)

'There are many more people attending now. The biggest difference I can see between then and now is in the clothes worn on Sunday – they were much more formal when I was younger. However, I don't think behaviour has changed much, although there is less respect for others – until grace intervenes.

'There were more visitors back and fore to each other's homes in those days, and this was a good source of fellowship.

'There was no crèche until Rev Kenny MacDonald's time as

minister – Granny would baby-sit, and later on the older child
would look after the younger ones.' (EM)

'Parents took turns at staying home with the young children
until they were of the age to sit and appreciate and respect that
they were in God's house and had to be on their best behaviour.'
(JP)

'In Church, there was usually a good congregation and I think
the singing was good too. For many years Johnny MacKenzie
was the precentor. Then Mr Ross, Glasgow House, came to the
village, and he also became a precentor. He had a very powerful
voice. The "Handers" family of girls were also singers – so the
precentor got help from that area of the church.' (JMI)

'As far back as I can remember, our church was always
blessed with men who could lead the singing. That is still the
case today. One man who precented in our church wrote a psalm
tune, "Ardross". On the subject of musical composition, a nephew
of Maggie the Mason (who had a house close to the church)
composed a pipe tune called "Achnagarron". He was a bagpipe
reed-maker in Glasgow. The name of the tune was later changed
to "The Queen's Welcome".

'Gaelic services were held in the church until 1937 or 1938.
Both Gaelic and English services were taken by Rev John
MacDonald. Gaelic services were held at 11am and English
followed.' (AGM)

On Communion Sundays, Mrs Jean MacKay would go out
from church an hour before the service finished (as members
went forward to the tables). She would then walk up to the manse
and get lunch ready. She recalls a big spread of food for the
ministers and elders.

There were fewer people who sat at the Communion tables
in Jean's youth than nowadays. The congregation as a whole is
also much bigger now.

'Evening services were held in the Perrins Road Hall, as there
was no electricity in the church.

'On Communion days no-one approached the tables at the

first singing – only at the singing of the second psalm was the first move made.

'Once a month, Rev MacDonald went to Ardross in the evening to preach there. On that occasion, an elder took the evening service in Alness. There were two elders who came time about – Mr John Reid and Mr Donald Ross. On these occasions we had them for dinner. They both had farms eastwards from the church. I've just been wondering, how did they get home at night, especially in the winter time? We are so busy doing our own thing when young that we don't ask the questions we would now like answered!' (JMI)

One woman who grew up in Ardross at the time of Mr MacDonald's ministry is Mrs Alex Allison. She was born at Loanreach and baptised at home, not in the church, by the United Free Minister, Rev John Ross.

'At that time very few in the area did not go to the local church – and everyone walked. The Allisons and others headed down to the Free Church in Rosskeen in traps for the morning service. Some went down to Rosskeen again for the evening service, but she went to Sunday School at Ardross Church at 5pm and the service which followed at 6pm.

'There were four or five teachers in the Sunday School and nearly thirty children. The minister taking the service went into the Sunday School and sang a psalm or hymn with the children, said a prayer and had a talk with them. The teachers in the Sunday School were from all three denominations represented.

'The established church minister (Rev D McDairmaid) did two services and the United Free and Free Church ministers (Rev J Ross and Rev John MacDonald) each took one service of the month. If there was a fifth Sunday, the United Free minister usually did it. There was great unity and co-operation between the denominations, while still paying respect to church traditions, e.g. FC services sang only psalms while UF services sang both psalms and hymns.

'There was a committee for the church – all three ministers being trustees.

'Mr Perrins gave the church to the community as a thanks offering for the recovery of his wife after an illness. It was for all employees on his estate. He also gave a Christmas tree to the community which went into the small hall at Dublin. It was in a field in front of the houses, all of which contained estate employees. The hall was a community hall and was used for playing billiards. During the war the military took it over and it was lost to the people, so a new hall was built.

'Alness Parish Church was in the cemetery at Alness. At one time it had two ministers – Martin and Laidler. They went up to the Boath school and took services there. People also came from both Boath and Kildermorie to the Ardross Church. The church was full then. There was a big Free Church representation in Strathy – Stewarts, Rosses, Grahams and MacKenzies.'

**Running the church**
'The Finance Committee of bygone days decided what was to be done about the Church, and with the money.

'A random roll-call (with apologies to those missed out) would include these names: Rod MacGregor, Willie MacLean (the cottages), Dan MacIntosh (Newmore), Jimmy MacDonald (Newmore), Willie Tuach, John MacKenzie (Achnagarron) and the other John MacKenzie (who also precented), Davie MacLeod and his father, D W Ross, Kenny MacIver (Snr), Robertson Dallas, Willie Ross (Tomich), John Ross, Sollie Peterkin, Hugh Sutherland, Roy Harmon, George Dryden and, I think, Christie Allison (Stittenham) and Pete Ross, Duncan Stewart and John Murchison (Bridgend).

'To add to the money collected in the plate on the Sabbath, people used to go round the districts twice yearly with the Sustentation Collection Book. You wrote your name and address and the amount you were giving: Miss Georgie MacKay, Mossfield, collected for our area. Mr George MacLeod, Bridgend

School, later introduced the envelope system, and the proceeds from it covered a'thing.' (AGM)

In 1890 a legacy had been received known as The MacKay bequest from a Mrs Ellen MacKay of Uddingston, who was originally from the Ardross area. The conditions were that the interest, which was about £15 per annum, was to be used to assist the poor of the Parish of Rosskeen. The capital was invested in a Land Company from Edinburgh, which appears to have gone out of business in 1908 with the loss of our money. However, the bequest was continued with the money coming from the General Fund of the Congregation until 1970 when due to changing circumstances and conditions it was closed.

'The Sustentation Fund Meeting and also the Women's Foreign Mission Meetings were both held in the manse. After it was all collected, the collectors gathered at the manse. This was always followed by a lovely tea.' (JM)

'When I look back over those who undertook duties in the church I find I can remember the names of the five who were treasurers in my time. They were: John Ross (Seaforth), D W Ross, George MacLeod (Bridgend School), John Kennedy (Royal Bank of Scotland, Invergordon) and Roy Harmon – the latter having to deal with a greatly increased workload.' (AGM)

'In Mr MacDonald's time, the elders were: Donald Ross (Stoneyfield), John Ross (Seaforth), Davie Graham, Rory MacKenzie (Newbridge) and the deacon was Kenneth Stewart.' (JP)

## Heating

'My mother, Mrs Winchester, was church cleaner for eleven years (1917-1928). On Sunday mornings she used to walk down from Mossfield to light the fires in the two vestries. I remember my brother going along to help. During Communions, the two fires were kept on throughout Thursday to Monday without going out at all.

'The volunteer for taking care of the boiler-house was Mr

Doddy MacKenzie, Achnagarron (father of Mr A G MacKenzie).' (J.P.)

'The heating system in the church was made by Rose Street Foundry, Inverness (now A I Welders). It was known as "The Heating Apparatus".

'When the coal was of good quality, and the wind in the right direction on the church, you could hear the water thumping powerfully in the pipes during the sermon.

'My grandfather, Sandy MacKenzie, looked after the heating in the church until he died in 1916. My father then took over and carried on till about the beginning of the Second World War, by which time the system was beginning to show signs of its age. Just before the war, coal was rationed and scarce. In the winter of 1936-37, there were seven weeks of severe frost. Father had to attend to the fire three times a day to keep the pipes from bursting. This took a lot of time.

'A great amount of work went into heating the building. For instance, in ordinary weather the ashes from the previous Sunday had to be cleaned out on the Saturday. The fire had to be set for lighting at 11pm. Then you sat for about an hour to make sure the fire burned up. When you were sure, you put more coal on to keep the fire going until 7am on Sunday. At that point you raked out the ashes and put fresh coal on to keep the fire right till 11am. Twelve hours after lighting the fire, you went in and gave it a poke up, hoping all the while that the church would be warm. As I remember it, three to four cwts of coal were burned each weekend!

'The church was not heated during the war years as the sermons were held in the top and bottom vestries. The partition was opened up and both fires were put on. The place got quite warm, but people tried to avoid sitting beside either fire, as their left legs got burned.

'My father did finally give up the church heating for a variety of reasons, one being the amount of time it took up.

'After the war, some of the church heating pipes burst in a

frost due to some water having gathered in the low-level pipes. This was repaired, and Rod Cameron, who worked in the Smiddy, and stayed, conveniently, in a home in front of the Old Manse, now no longer there, took on the heating job.

'But the spreaders in the heating coils started to collapse. When the spreaders did collapse, it became impossible to heat the church. A replacement heating system had to be found.

'Relevant to this, the coil system in Lairg Free Church heating apparatus had broken down some time before. A new coil had to be made in Aberdeen. The cost of this was £100.00, plus the work costs for three days of three men, of whom I was one. The Rosskeen Finance Committee decided this was too dear. It was decided to heat the church by gas. But the hot air rose and tended to go through a vent in the church ceiling, and then out through the vent on top of the roof. There was talk of lowering the ceiling inside the church to save the heat.

'The centre vent on top of the church is now only part of its original height. The middle section became rusted and blew off in a gale many years ago. The top section was still in reasonable condition, so a Polish workman, employed by Ross & Ross, Masons, Alness, put the top section back on.' (AGM)

### Doorkeepers and Bell ringers

'One of the psalms speaks of the psalmist's wish to be a doorkeeper in God's house. In days gone by, in our church (as in other Free Churches), some of the men who stood at the church door were not office-bearers or even members, possibly because there were too few of these. The rota system now in the church has brought order into this duty, so that no-one need feel unnerved going into God's house.

'The church bell which rings today was cast by John Warner & Sons, London in 1899. The earliest bellringers I can remember are Alistair MacDonald, the Manse, and John MacKenzie, known as Johnny Mount Misery, who also precented, and who had to scuttle down from the bell-tower with perfect timing in order to take his seat in the precentor's box at the very moment when D W Ross, the other precentor, led the minister into the pulpit from the vestry.

'The last bellringer I remember before the war was Alastair Ross, D W Ross's son, before he went off to the RAF, and later became a minister.

'I remember Simon Ross, the wood, keeping the ground outside the church tidy. Simon was Ken Ross, the bicycle agent's father.

'I can also remember John Ross (Jondan) looking after the church and its surroundings.

'Mrs Reid (Jessie Gallie's mother) and Mrs Reid's mother both used to clean the church and set the fires (as did Mrs Jenny Peterkin's mother, already mentioned). Jessie's father used to cut the grass and Dutch-hoe the weeds, as did David and Walter MacLeod's father, and also Jimmy MacDonald.

'As always has been the way, ministers, office-bearers, members and adherents in a church rise up, have their day, and die out. One elder, whose piety and sincere Christian character the older people used to vouch for, was Donald Ross, Stoneyfield, who died in November 1931. His son, Alex Ross, who was a member in Rev Hugh MacCallum's time told me of the most grievous experience his father ever had.

'On 30th December 1915, Donald Ross was clipping turnip up at Stoneyfield and taking them to the pit with the horse and cart. He heard some very funny noises, and looked eastward to see the HMS Natal upend herself in the sea, and slowly settle beneath the water. The experience moved him profoundly.'

Donald Ross's sudden death on Sabbath 22nd November 1931 'produced a great blank in the parish of Rosskeen', according to his obituary, written for the *Ross-shire Journal* by Mr William Ross (commonly known as 'Willie the Blaster'). 'The large number of persons and of motor cars… was a very trustworthy indication of the very high esteem in which he was meritoriously held over a large area of country.' He continues: 'The late Donald

Ross.... learned much in the school of experience, and lived an industrious life. There is no exaggeration in the affirmation that he was a good farmer, a loving husband, and an amiable and wise farmer, and a man who wished to love his neighbour as himself.

'That is a great character, and its reality was the efflorescence in life of his Christian faith, which was sincere and strong. An esteemed elder in Rosskeen Free Church, his immediate fellow-workers must be allowed to know his ability, his earnestness, and his untiring perseverance in assisting every goodly object that came within his sphere. I feel sure that his sudden removal by death is profoundly felt by all his fellow-workers, as a great loss sustained by them, and many in the surrounding parishes join with them in this feeling.

'I cannot withhold the remark that, within a brief period of time, many persons have been removed by death from the upper parts of the parishes of Rosskeen and Logie Easter. God is speaking to us in His dispensations, and I hear, as it were, the climax in the book of providence during the latter few months, and I realise in some measure, however inadequately, that, to me, the "term" is drawing nigh, and the "flitting" will soon be.

'Let me closely examine myself with regard to my "lamp". Is it well trimmed, having oil, and brightly burning? Still further, let me be sure of having some supply of "oil" for, without it, I will be undone in my pilgrimage.

'I allude to Christ's parable of the Ten Virgins, which finds place in Matthew 25 vs 1-13, which I wish the reader of these remarks to read. Bengel wrote some remarks about this subject, which I like very much, and I simply hand them round. The "fire" of the lamps represents the gracious light, warmth and purification, which we passively receive from the Spirit of God; but the "oil" is what must be obtained by diligent prayer, and in faithful obedience in the way of nourishing and increasing this light, warmth and purification. Calvin has aptly remarked that, it is not enough once to be prepared for our duty, unless we continue to the end. I may safely affirm the late Mr Donald Ross kept his "lamp" burning to the end of his earthly pilgrimage' (contributed by AGM).

What a debt we owe today to the faithful prayers and lives of our spiritual forbears.

Rev John MacDonald died on 22nd April 1947 aged eighty-five years. He served as minister at Rosskeen for thirty-nine years. A plaque on the pulpit wall of Rosskeen Church today reads:

'In memory of the late Rev John MacDonald. Born 1861. Died 1947. Ordained to the gospel ministry in 1891, he loyally served the Free Church of Scotland in the congregations of:

Acharacle  for  4 years

Raasay  for  15 years

Rosskeen  for  39 years

He was appointed Moderator of the General Assembly in 1915. A conscientious and uncompromising supporter of reformation principles, he greatly helped maintain the witness of the Free Church of Scotland during the 1900 Union controversy. An able theologian, diligent pastor, faithful preacher and devoted friend, his departure is greatly lamented.

'Blessed are the dead who die in the Lord'.

Revelation 14:13.

# CHAPTER 3

## REV JOHN R MUIRDEN

'The Rev John R Muirden MA was inducted to the pastorate of
the congregation of Rosskeen in 1948. A son of the Rev and Mrs
George Muirden, Free Church Minister of the Maryburgh
congregation, his early years were spent in the parish of Tarbat,
Easter Ross, where his father ministered before his translation
to the charge of Maryburgh. When the family moved to
Maryburgh, John Muirden attended Dingwall Academy. His
academic achievements at this school and afterwards at Aberdeen
University, where he graduated in Arts, were of the order that
could be expected from one whose intelligence was remarkably
keen and comprehensive. Having finished his Theological Course
at the Free Church College in 1940, he was ordained and inducted
to the charge of Maryburgh as successor to his father, and there
he ministered for eight years' (The Monthly Record).

A call addressed to him from the congregation of Rosskeen in
1948 was accepted.

The *Ross-shire Journal* reported the induction thus:

'The Free Church of Rosskeen, erected and gifted by the
munificence of a private donor, is probably the finest rural
ecclesiastical edifice in the Highlands. Beautifully situated in
its rural seclusion, the church ministers to the needs not only of
an extensive agricultural area, but of the communities of
Invergordon and Alness.

'Long before the hour appointed for the opening of the
ceremony, crowds could be seen assembling by foot, car, bicycle

44

and bus. Among these were a number of friends from the Maryburgh congregation and a goodly representation from Dingwall.

'Rev D Leitch, MA, Free Church Dingwall, the last inducted minister in the Presbytery, presided over a large gathering, and conducted the services, delivering a weighty and solemn address, based appropriately on the text: 'These men are servants of the most high God, which show unto us the way of salvation.' After the customary questions had been put and answered, the members of the Presbytery extended the right hand of fellowship to Mr Muirden on his admission to the charge.

'Rev Norman Campbell, senior minister of Dingwall, addressed the newly inducted minister on his pastoral and pulpit duties, emphasising the need of deep study of the Word for his public ministrations and for his own spiritual edification. The Rev D MacLeay, Fearn, delivered the charge to the congregation.

'At this point in the proceedings the customary presentations were made, the Rev D Leitch temporarily vacating the chair in favour of the Rev S MacIver, interim moderator in the vacancy. Mr J Ross, in handing to Mr Muirden a wallet of notes, had many interesting reminiscences to narrate of former pastorates in their area from the days of the ministry of Mr Carment onwards, and of eras of spiritual blessing and uplift their congregation had witnessed. On behalf of the Sabbath School, Master A Munro presented Mr Muirden with a gift from the juvenile members. Mr Muirden feelingly replied, thanking the congregation for their kindness and for the gracious reception and welcome they had accorded him.

'Mrs Murchison, Schoolhouse, Alness, in the name of the congregation, made a presentation to Mr Donald Ross, Glasgow House, Alness, in recognition of his highly valued and much appreciated services during the vacancy. Mr Ross, after replying with his wonted fervour and eloquence, was called on to present a gift to the Rev S MacIver, retiring moderator, for the painstaking and worthy service he had rendered to the congregation.'

Rev John A MacDonald (who was called home to be with his Lord on Saturday 19th October 1996 at the ripe old age of ninety-nine years) spent thirty-two years of his ministry as Free Church minister of the neighbouring parish of Kiltearn. Although at the time they were in different Presbyteries, Rev John Muirden was his nearest Free Church colleague. He wrote of him: 'He was in several respects a remarkable man. Apart from his gifts as a theological scholar, he was unique in several other respects. In some ways he was able to foretell future events. For example, before the events occurred, he dreamt that President Roosevelt had died and was succeeded by a Mr Truman – a name that was totally strange to him. The scenes of his dreams were identical to what he was to witness when fully awake. Even the dresses of the ladies he saw at weddings in his dreams were identical to what they were at the various gatherings when they came to pass.

'Not only as a theologian and a preacher did he excel. He was also an expert at woodwork. Puppets he made were much admired for their appearance and design.

'I heard him lauded by a Professor from Aberdeen, of which University Mr Muirden was a graduate.

'In losing him, I lost my best friend, and today I have reason to thank God for the privilege of knowing him.'

Mr Muirden's daughter, Anne, remembers that friendship well. "My father and Mr MacDonald were very close friends. They shared a common interest in fishing, and used to go away for a day's fishing to one of the remoter lochs in Ross-shire or Sutherland."

Anne remembers attending, with her brother, the Sabbath School in the church at 11am. There were not many children, but they came from the area around the church. She recalls a "girl who cycled from Inchindoun, some miles away – something one would not expect a child to do today. There was also a Sunday School in Alness and one in Ardross. When we lived in the old manse, the house and surrounding area were rather different even from today. The manse stood on its own grounds with a few cottages round about. It still bore signs of its former glory. There was an orchard and a vegetable garden, an area with a disused well, a barn, laundry, henhouse, byre and a stable for two horses. The glebe was let out to a local farmer for grazing. The manse had twelve rooms, including the maid's bedroom up the back stairs from the scullery. We didn't have all the rooms furnished, of course, and there was no heating in those days. I remember getting up on a winter's morning and scraping the frost off the inside of the window to see if there was snow or not! When my parents married, and came to live there, there was no electricity, but it was installed soon afterwards. The kitchen was some way from the dining-room and I remember my mother carrying trays of soup plates along the corridor, especially at Communion time. We eventually, however, had quite a modern kitchen. The huge beech tree which stands at the bottom of the old manse was planted by Mrs MacDonald – the former lady of the manse.'

Anne has a photograph of her father 'admiring' the Calor Gas heating system which was installed, in the early 50s, before the present system. The gas heaters were lit with a long pole, with a piece of cotton wool on the end, which had been soaked in meths.

At Mr Muirden's first Communion, Mrs Ena MacIver became his first communicant member, and Mr Sollie and Mrs Jenny Peterkin went forward at his second Communion into his ministry. Jenny's late husband Sollie was a firm favourite with young and old. The unofficial 'office' that Sollie held from the 1940s was 'doorkeeper' in Rosskeen Church. The warmth of Sollie's welcome was later borne out by reference being made to this 'office' at his funeral service, when, contrary to the normal procedure at the close of such a service, the door used to convey the remains from the church was affectionately referred to by Rev Kenny MacDonald as 'Sollie's Door'.

From Mr Muirden's ministry, Sollie was 'doorkeeper', then in Rev John L MacKay's time Sollie's duties included keeping a count of the number of people attending the morning service. During the ministry of Rev Kenny MacDonald, Sollie's duties were extended to welcoming folk at the Alness hall for the evening service and at the mid-week Prayer Meeting. Ill health was the contributing factor which finally saw Sollie giving up this service to the Lord.

Jenny Peterkin remembers Mr Muirden holding Friday Communion service in the Mason's Hall in Invergordon. In the late 1960s, Mr Muirden also held a Gaelic Communion service in the Alness Hall. Mr MacLeod, Headmaster, was expected to precent for this service, but due to ill-health had to stand down, and Mr Neil MacLeod, Dingwall, precented instead. It was hoped to repeat this Gaelic service, but sadly Mr Muirden's own health prevented this.

The twice yearly door-to-door collections for the Sustentation Fund continued, and both the Sustentation Fund Meeting and the Women's Foreign Mission Meeting continued to be held in the manse.

The regular services were the two on Sunday and the mid-week Prayer Meeting, and the Sunday School Picnic and the Winter Party remained the two congregational outings.

'The china cups and saucers, the white ones with red spots, were purchased from Woolworths by Mr MacLeod, Headmaster at Bridgend Primary, who was an elder at Rosskeen. This was the first of Rosskeen's own crockery to be gathered in. Before this if tea was necessary, folks took their own, with one or two of the ladies taking extra china to cover any who had none. The bread plates were also collected around the same time by donations from the ladies of the congregation. Some of these are still in use to this present day.' (JP)

The red-spotted cups are also still going strong, now providing refreshment at regular and frequently packed gatherings in the Church Hall!

'In Mr Muirden's time, notice came from the Assembly for the baptisms to be held in the church. Up until this point, baptisms were normally held in the home. Mr Muirden's first baptism saw five babies baptised: Donald Ross, Uisdean Duff, Sheana MacIver, Catherine MacKinnon and a baby MacKenzie.

For home baptisms, Mr Muirden took his elders with him to the parents' house. The elders during Mr Muirden's ministry were Mr Donald Ross, Glasgow House; Mr MacKenzie, Invergordon; Donnie Bruce; Kenny MacIver, Alness and Davie MacLeod, Alness.' (JP)

Mr Stuart Cameron, now a resident of Maryburgh, has family connections with Rosskeen. He and his brother Ronnie attended Sunday School from 1950-59, during which time his father and mother were both communicant members.

'My father Roddie was church officer and beadle from 1952-57. He also rang the bell, and the congregation knew if someone else was ringing it as he had a distinctive tone. He always started the bell at 11.45, until 3 minutes past 12. He would take his jacket off, place his pocket watch on the window-sill and time it. He also cleaned the belfry. I remember once when the rope broke, he went up the wooden ladder attached to the wall, re-attached the rope, and oiled the flywheel and clapper. Mr Muirden did not want him to go up as he was frightened he would fall. He also cleaned the church and lit the coal-fired stove on the Saturday night, and banked it up. It would still be going on the Sunday morning, and would be restoked to heat the church for the morning service.'

Mr Roy and Mrs Katie Harmon came to Rosskeen in 1953, to 'a warm welcome', Mrs Harmon says. 'The congregation was mixed – made up of some old, some middle-aged and a good many young folk. In those days everyone came to church clean and tidy in their Sunday clothes – no jeans or dungarees! They were very hard times of unemployment and low wages, but in spite of that, nobody complained.

'There was no crèche then – children stayed with their parents, and they were always very well-behaved in church.

'Most people still walked or cycled in the fifties, or got lifts from those who owned cars. We all looked forward to the Communions, and the good preachers we always had. I remember a number of services really well by Mr Muirden, Mr MacCallum, John MacKay and Kenny MacDonald. I don't remember any Gaelic services.

'We always enjoyed the Outings we had to Nigg Bay, Shandwick Bay, Portmahomack, Ardross and the Black Isle. There were no behaviour problems in those days. I would like to see more reverence and respect for others. Nothing works without order and discipline, and I would like to see more of it in God's House.

'People could always sit where they wanted, but families tended to stick to the same pew for years. This did make for good order, as no-one needed to run around looking for a seat at the last minute.'

Mr Roy Harmon has given many years of service since then to the Lord and to the congregation, as treasurer and later also as clerk to the Deacon's Court. Mr Harmon's gifts are perfectly suited to these responsibilities which involve a great deal of meticulous record-keeping. We all owe him our grateful appreciation.

Another family which has long had connections with Rosskeen are the MacIver family from Alness. Mr Kenny MacIver, who served as an elder since Mr Muirden's day, is fondly remembered, and has been greatly missed since his death in November 1980. His widow, Mrs Ena MacIver, remembers one occasion when there was a particularly severe snowstorm, which meant that only the Peterkins and the MacIvers, as well as Mr Muirden were able to get to church. Because of the conditions, Mr Muirden and Kenny MacIver prayed, and then everyone returned home. Kenny and Ena had ten children, seven of whom still live locally and are very involved with Rosskeen Church. Two of them, Hugh and Mhairi (MacLeod), looked back for us to their time growing up under Mr Muirden's ministry.

Mhairi remembers attending church when she was about five. 'Sundays were extra special – always family days. We walked to the morning service at Rosskeen from our home in Alness – the evening one being held in the Alness Hall. We walked regardless of the weather conditions – occasionally getting a lift from Mr Murchison or Mr Pete Ross (the painter). There were very few cars then. After church, it was home for dinner and then help with the dishes before setting off for Sunday School in the afternoon. At Sunday School we were told Bible stories and then discussed the story. We repeated our psalms, Bible verses and the catechism. Our teachers were Mr Murchison, who was our headmaster, and Mr MacIver, who was my father – so behaviour had to be impeccable!

'We came home then, to do our Sunday School lessons, having a wee rest before heading off to church again. Home again, and after tea we had evening worship before going to bed.

'Our home was always a meeting place. I used to love when we would sit round the fire with our late elders – Mr D Bruce, Mr David MacLeod and his father Mr John MacLeod, and Mr D W Ross. We would sing psalms and pray together.

'The number of church attenders was fewer than today, and there were no children under five years old because there was no crèche. Mothers stayed at home in the morning or evening until the children were about five. Instead of women meeting together for prayer and Bible Studies during the weekdays, as we do today, women studied privately at home.'

Mhairi's brother, Hugh MacIver, now an elder, remembers that an evening service was held in Ardross and Invergordon on alternate weeks.

'Family worship morning and evening consisted of singing, reading and prayer. After church, it was dinner, then off to Sunday School at 3pm. We were not allowed out to play, or to go for

walks. In good weather the family would lie out on the green at
the back of the house and read books.'

The Sunday School teachers Hugh had were Jenny Peterkin,
Davie MacLeod, Dolly MacKenzie, Kenny MacIver (Hugh's
dad) and Mr Muirden. Hugh remembers getting reprimanded
from Mr Muirden for bending his Bible over!

The greatest difference he sees between attending church
today and earlier days at Rosskeen, is that church life is more
informal now. This means that people find it easier to talk about
spiritual things, and are more willing to do so. However, he
wonders if perhaps people are not so well versed in the Scriptures
as they used to be.

Mrs Hansi Sutherland recalls:

'We came to live in Invergordon in 1954. Davine was four
years old and Ross was born a few months later. At that time Mr
Muirden was minister of Rosskeen Free Church and he started
to hold a Sunday School class himself in the local primary school
for the Invergordon Free Church children.

'Nothing much sticks in my memory of the years the kids
were growing up. Sunday School outings were always looked
forward to, usually to places with lovely sandy beaches like
Shandwick, Portmahomack and Rosemarkie – lots of room and
freedom to let off high spirits. One outing in particular I
remember. That was to Shandwick Bay and for the first time I
can recall, there was a ladies race – all ages – along the hard
sand of the bay. To our own surprise, and no doubt everyone
else's, Mrs Harmon and I finished first, neck-and-neck a couple
of lengths ahead of the field. I wouldn't like to try that now!

'Still on those early years, I remember Mr Muirden on a visit
once telling us about the many little things to be observed from
the pulpit. One Sunday during the sermon he was very amused
to notice the MacLeod bairns at the back of the middle row having
a "foot race" up the back of the pew in front. As the heads and
shoulders slid down and disappeared, pairs of feet appeared on

the ledge. That little ploy got short shift! That pulpit is a great vantage point; perhaps even the odd surreptitious sweetie popped in during the sermon doesn't go un-noticed.

'Then there was the great day of the cleaning of the church. That would have been about 1965 I think. Most of the able-bodied in the congregation turned out with pails, brooms, scrubbers, soap etc. and the church got its biggest spring-clean ever. We all had jobs and areas allocated – floors were scrubbed, pews dusted and polished, every corner that could be reached was dealt with, every cobweb got a hurry. When at last the job was done the whole interior sparkled. Outside the men had been hard at work too, cleaning out rone-pipes and gutters and raking gravel. It was a most satisfactory communal effort, all done with great goodwill and plenty of humour and laughter.

'One more early memory stands out. In 1967 a sale of work was held to raise funds towards the heating and re-decoration of the church. I think it was about the biggest and best of its kind that I've ever attended. Its organising alone must have been a tremendous feat. The sale was held in Alness old Town Hall and the amount and variety of the stuff donated was amazing. You name it, we had it. Bags and boxes of farm produce of all kinds, dozens of cartons of eggs, jams, preserves, fruit, flowers, pot plants etc. The trestles were groaning under the weight. As usual, the baking stall was the biggest magnet. Right in the middle was an enormous clootie-duff, so big it had to be sold off in slices. Stalls with books, handicrafts, ornaments and bits of furniture filled the space round walls and the whole upstairs was devoted to jumble. A great deal of that was children's clothing and with not much money around in those days mothers and kids just made a bee-line for the stairs. I believe there was very little left of it when the sale was over. People came from all over Easter Ross and the hall was jam-packed for hours. The final sum raised was £440.12s., which was a really handsome figure for those days, and was almost half of the total amount needed to install the heating and lighting system (£953 plus) in the following year.'

## Rosskeen Free Church Sabbath School

'I came into Rosskeen Free Church Sabbath School in August
1962, following a visit from Mr Muirden who explained that
there would be an addition to the manse family in the autumn,
and the situation required someone to help him with the morning
Sunday Schools, one in the church at 11am and the other in the
Alness Hall at 3pm, each Sunday.

'The Alness Sunday School was quite separate from the one
in the church. I didn't know much about it, but I understood it
was run by our late elders, Kenny MacIver and Davie MacLeod.
They were in charge from 1954 to 1964. For long periods, they
were helped by Mrs Jenny Peterkin who also worked with me in
Alness from 1966 summer holidays till Christmas 1968.

'Mr Muirden presided over the Church Sunday School. He
and the teacher helping him occupied opposite corners of the
building. Lessons began punctually. If there was a delay, early
arrivals for the service came tramping in, and then followed the
indignities of having to rush the lesson, and after that departing
scholars got mixed up with the arriving congregation. Most of
the children came on foot or on bicycles from the farm cottages
around us. There were sufficient numbers of workers on these
farms for the numbers in the Sunday School to be not far short
of the numbers there now. Pupils over the age of nine went to
Mr Muirden. Below nine, they stayed with the teacher helping
him. Mr Muirden began by singing part of a psalm, praying, and
then he and I went to our respective corners. Few of the Sunday
School pupils waited for the service at 12 o'clock. Nevertheless,
some of these youngsters had learned enough in the Sunday
School to gain places in the Welfare of Youth Examination.

'Time, however moved on. Most of the pupils in the church
outgrew Sunday School. Kenny and Davie intimated their
intention of giving up the Sunday School work in Alness. Mr
Muirden decided that the two Sunday Schools should merge,
and there would be one Sunday School only, in mid-afternoon,
in the Alness Hall. Mr Muirden came down one July evening in

1964 to ask me to take charge of the combined Sunday School in Alness. I took the work on with some trepidation, but I knew that I had gained experience from teaching 16 and 17 year olds in the Glasgow Church of Scotland Sunday School, where there were hundreds of pupils. My work in the Alness Hall went on till early 1970. I remember being grateful to Anne Muirden during the year she was with me because she was musical and she and the MacIver family kept the psalm singing on the right lines, at the beginning of each lesson.' (Dolly MacKenzie)

### Alina's Story

'We moved to Alness on my seventh birthday. Mr MacDonald was the minister and he seemed very very old. I remember his gracious manner and kindly words. We sat well forward and it was impossible to see the clock without very obviously turning round! We were never given sweets with noisy wrappers – but two "buttermints" and a "pandrop" lasted for the duration of most services.

'Following Mr MacDonald's death we had a variety of preachers. Mr Gunn, a shepherd, and Mr Thomas Boag, a grocer, were two laymen who came quite often to preach when the need arose. Our father started up the Sunday School following the morning service. It was a case of learning a verse of a psalm, and a catechism and listening to a Bible story. Once a year we had the "Welfare of Youth" examinations and during the summer the Sunday School Picnic. I remember one or two Christmas – or New Year – parties in the Alness Hall. The Communion Season was a special time and even although we were young we attended all the meetings. I remember one elderly lady from Ardross who used to weep at the Lord's table and I used to wonder what it was that moved her so much.

'We used to enjoy the experience of visiting other congregations at their Communion season – and also the Annual Strathpeffer Convention.

'The Presbytery planned a week of special meetings at which

the guest preacher was Rev Kenneth MacRae, Stornoway. We travelled to the various venues by chartered bus. It was at one of these meetings that I was converted at the age of eleven (or so). Mr MacRae preached that night on Revelation 22:17 "And the Spirit and the bride say, Come. And let him that heareth say, Come. And let him that is athirst come. And whosoever will, let him take the water of life freely". I wept that night for the sheer joy of knowing that my sins had been forgiven and that through faith in Jesus I am guaranteed a place in heaven.

'I was about fourteen when I was challenged to be at the Lord's table. My mother was unsure and one of her questions was, "Are you willing to break with the world?"' That probably meant foregoing the Christmas Guide and Scout Party and the School Dance. Having convinced her that I was, I 'met the Session', and was graciously welcomed by Mr Muirden. We used to go forward to the Communion Table singing Psalm 118, 'O set ye open unto me the gates of righteousness..'. These were happy days and the whole day was the Lord's. Following a special Sunday lunch (cooked the previous evening) we read good books and very often had a psalm or hymn singing session. My father and I rounded up some of the children who lived near the Alness hall and we started a little Sunday School for them.

'The Sunday evening service alternated in time – one week at 4.30pm and the next week at 5pm – depending on whether there was a service in Ardross or not. I was sent each Sunday to make sure "Mrs Bain" had the right time. She was a good Christian whose husband used to drink and who didn't encourage her attendance at church. Following treatment for cancer she was unable to come – so instead I used to visit and sing with her. I have precious memories of singing with her the Sunday before she died. She told me that she knew that "Alex" (Mr Bain) would be saved. My father and I continued to visit him on Sunday evenings and he very soon began to attend church and to pray for himself. He was a changed man. I think he must have been about eighty!

'Following a visit of the Rev John Murdo MacLeod with the "Highways and Byways" caravan I started visiting an old lady on Sunday nights and reading and praying with her. She had no church connections and I don't know whether she ever truly believed. But looking back, although we weren't pushed into evangelism – we were never discouraged – and I am very grateful for these early days in Rosskeen Church where we benefited from Mr Muirden's preaching and godly example. I marvel too at the wisdom of our parents who in their own quiet way encouraged us and gave us opportunity to be about the Master's business.'

'Only one life, it will soon be past,
only what's done for Christ will last.'

(Mrs Alina MacKenzie, Glasgow.)

The statement of Accounts for the year ending 31st December 1966 includes the following information:

Finance

Total Income – £1,341:19: 4
Total Expenditure – £1,328:10: 9

(These are detailed on the Statement).

Sabbath Services:-

| | |
|---|---|
| Morning – Church (at Achnagarron) | at 12 o'clock |
| Evening – Free Church Hall (Alness) | at 5pm |
| Sabbath School – Hall | at 3pm |
| Prayer Meeting – Hall | Wednesday at 7.30pm |

Elders: Messrs D Bruce, K MacIver, D MacLeod, G MacLeod, M.A.

Finance Committee: Rev J R Muirden, M.A., G MacLeod Esq. M.A. Secretary; Messrs D Bruce, K MacIver, D MacLeod, S Peterkin, W MacLean, R G MacGregor, W Ross, W MacLeod, D J MacLeod, R J Harmon, J Kennedy.

Sabbath School Teachers: Mrs MacKenzie, Superintendent; Anne Muirden.

The statement concludes with the following letter:

To the Members and Adherents of Rosskeen Free Church

The year of 1966, for the congregation, has been one to remember. During more than half of it, I was ill and unable to undertake any of my duties. In all this I was very conscious of your concern, your sympathy and your good wishes, and these helped me greatly. I appreciate too your loyal continued support to the Church, both financially and in your attendance at the services during this past difficult year. I gladly take this opportunity of thanking you all and of asking your continued support and your continued prayers.

10th Jan, 1967
John R Muirden.

Mr Muirden died at his home on Wed. 21st August 1968, at the age of 52 years. His obituary, which appeared in *The Monthly Record*, reads:

'Mr Muirden was a man of many parts and his administrative ability and business acumen, as also his able pen, were used in the best interests of the community in which Providence placed him. His chief concern, however, was the cause of the gospel and its welfare. His talents were truly dedicated to Christ. On various Committees of the Church and as a clerk of Synod and Presbytery for many years, he gave valuable and ungrudging service. But it can be said that his preaching and pastoral duties were that part of the work in which he found greatest satisfaction. For him, the preaching of the gospel of his Lord and Saviour was a labour of love. Thoroughly versed in the doctrines of the Reformed Faith, his expositions of Scripture were warmly evangelical and had a spiritual and edifying quality. A good command of language and lucid style enhanced the usefulness of all his pulpit work. He was a workman who needed not to be ashamed, rightly dividing the Word of Truth.

'The righteous hath hope in his death,' but the sorrow occasioned by the removal of God's people from this earthly scene is not for this reason less real. Being what they were, the grief experienced by all those who cherished their worth and companionship is all the more poignant. The grievous sense of loss, therefore, which was felt by the passing of the late Rev John R Muirden is understandable, for he was a man greatly beloved.

A man of impressive personality, and of gracious disposition, his genial presence will be missed in the homes of his people and in the whole community, as also in the courts of the church, where his influence was always a gracious one.

The funeral service was held on Sat. 24th August in the Free Church, Rosskeen, where many assembled from far and near. The service was conducted by Rev D MacLeay, Moderator of the Presbytery of Tain. Others taking part were Rev Prof. R A Finlayson, Rev J A MacDonald, Rev D Leitch, Rev C Graham and Rev D Ross.

The remains were laid to rest in the Rosskeen Cemetery. On the day following the funeral, the services in Rosskeen Free Church were conducted by Rev John A MacDonald, senior minister of Kiltearn Free Church. In paying tribute to the memory of a beloved friend and colleague, he said: "John Muirden was truly a man of God – a man who dearly loved his Saviour and took unfailing delight in the proclamation of his Master's gospel…. To know him was not only to respect, but also to love him. His gifts of heart and mind were such that one was irresistibly drawn to him, and in his presence one felt that this was indeed a friend on whose loyalty and judgement implicit confidence could be placed. We have abundant reason to thank God for every remembrance of him."

"Blessed are the dead which die in the Lord from henceforth:

Yea, saith the Spirit, that they may rest from their labours; and their works do follow them."   D Ross

In Rosskeen Church today, the plaque on the wall to the minister's right reads:

"In remembrance of the Rev John R Muirden M.A.
Born 1916 – Died 1968

Ordained to the ministry of the Free Church of Scotland in 1940. He loyally served the congregation of Maryburgh for 8 years and Rosskeen for 20 years. An able student of Scripture, he was wholehearted in his allegiance to Calvinistic theology and reformation principles.

A Devoted pastor and steadfast friend, who was esteemed by all.

Rev. XIV-13"

# CHAPTER 4

## REV HUGH MACCALLUM

Rev Hugh MacCallum was minister of Rosskeen from 1969 to 1979. Born and brought up in Ardnamurchan, Lochaber, he began studying for the ministry in 1964 – aged fifty years – a mature student. He first spent two years at Glasgow University as he had no formal qualifications, then attended the Free Church College from 1966-1969. During his time in the Free Church College he underwent major surgery for stomach ulcers, having two thirds of his stomach removed. His wife, Flora, left the family home in Caol, Fort William to live in the bedsit in Edinburgh to look after Hugh who needed a special diet after his operation. Leaving the family was a big wrench for both – it may even have been part of the cause of Mr MacCallum's ulcers, in addition to the stress of studies.

It must have been difficult for the two fifty year olds to adapt to student lifestyle – living on a grant, in one room, where they ate and slept, and shared a toilet with others in the house, who were also students, but younger. Hugh finished College in the summer of 1969.

Meanwhile, his son Aeneas had come up to work at the construction of the Smelter in Invergordon and told his parents of the beautiful church on the road to work. Mr MacCallum had never heard of Rosskeen! Apart from that, his only connection with the area was an acquaintance with Myra and Anne Matheson, who taught in Caol, Fort William. (Anne is now Anne Campbell, one of our Sunday School teachers.) Mrs Matheson had been down visiting her daughters and went back to Rosskeen and suggested Mr MacCallum to preach during the vacancy. He was ordained and inducted to Rosskeen in November 1969.

## Induction

Arriving at the manse on a very wintry night, the weather cold and dreich, they were faced with the task of organising furniture etc in their new home, when the phone rang. It was Willie and Margaret MacKenzie living in Novar, telling them to come for a meal, and that there were beds ready for them to stay overnight! Real divine provision! (Margaret and Willie had met in the MacCallum home in Caol and married in Kilmallie Free Church. They had left Caol to work in Auchterarder, Perthshire and moved to Evanton in August 1969.)

The induction took place on a very stormy night. The reception was held in Bridgend School.

Rev Duncan Leitch, Dingwall, preached Mr MacCallum 'in'. In the evening Mr MacCallum took the text in 1 Corinthians 2:2: 'For I determined not to know any thing among you, save Jesus Christ, and him crucified.' The lovely thing was that a friend, Rev Archibald MacDougall, sent a letter of encouragement, and in his letter he quoted the very text which Rev MacCallum had used for his first sermon. Such confirmation is a typically comforting assurance of the gentle leading of the Holy Spirit.

At the end of Mr Leitch's service, before the Benediction, Mr MacCallum asked that the congregation would give time for Mr Leitch and himself to get to the front door, as they wished to shake hands with the people on the way out. This habit continued, at Mr MacCallum's request, and so the hand-shaking at the door was introduced, and has continued until present time.

## New Year's Day Service

Mr MacCallum also introduced the New Year's Day Service. One particular New Year's Day happened to fall on a Wednesday, the day of the regular Prayer Meeting. Mr MacCallum put his idea to the elders, who agreed, and Mr Kenny MacIver, elder, suggested an 11am service in order to allow time for those who have dinners to prepare to do so. Mr MacCallum remembers the first service being well attended by the people.

## Outreach

When Nigg was a thriving workplace, there was a boat berthed in Nigg Harbour to provide accommodation for some of the workforce. At that time, Mr MacCallum, along with Rev K MacLeod, Tain, began outreach services to the Nigg workers. To date he does not know if anyone was reached by these attempts to spread the good news of Jesus.

## Schools

Mr MacCallum was also involved in the local schools. When he attended Invergordon Academy he did not take an assembly, as is done today, but was given time to spend with the Free Church children who attended the school. Some of his pupils he remembers were the MacGregor family, the Munro family (Commerce House), Morag and Catherine Ross from Delny Manse and Donald and Murdo MacIver.

Assemblies were taken in Park Primary School and in Bridgend Primary in Alness. In Park, the assemblies were shared with the Rev Sloan (Church of Scotland, Invergordon) and Father Bernard MacDonald. In Alness they were shared with Rev Howe (Church of Scotland).

## Dalmore House

The person in charge of Dalmore Home during Mr MacCallum's ministry was Mr Mounsey, and he went there to take a service on Tuesday evenings, perhaps once a month.

## Baptismal Font

The baptismal font was donated during Mr MacCallum's ministry by Mr Alastair MacGregor, in memory of his father, Mr Rod MacGregor.

## Office Bearers

When Mr MacCallum arrived in Rosskeen he had three elders: Mr Donnie Bruce, Mr Kenny MacIver, Mr Davie MacLeod.

During his ministry he had three more men added to the eldership: Mr Roy Harmon, Dr Callum MacAulay, and Mr Lindsay MacCallum. Mr David Wilkie was made a deacon.

Rev MacCallum encouraged more of the men to pray at the Prayer Meeting, especially some of the younger members.

## Communion

One particular memory Mr MacCallum has is of the June Communion in 1973, regarding Mrs Mhairi MacLeod who had been very faithful at the Prayer Meeting for quite some time. On the Saturday evening service Mhairi was there, but did not stay behind to make a profession of faith, as Rev MacCallum had hoped. On the way out, he asked her, 'Was she not staying?' She did not. However, she spent the whole night in tears and the following morning, before the service, her father, Mr Kenny MacIver, spoke with Rev MacCallum about his daughter's distress. A Session Meeting was called before the morning service to allow Mhairi to meet with them. The Session was made up of Rev MacCallum, Mr D Bruce, Mr D MacLeod and her father. Communion was taken by Principal Cameron, and there was rejoicing in heaven and upon the earth.

## Ardross Church

When Rev MacCallum arrived in Rosskeen he could not drive, so he got around the parish on his bike. He even went as far as Ardross on the bike!

In those days there was no-one to collect for the Leprosy Mission in Ardross, so he went on his bike around the area, making many valuable contacts outwith the Free Church folk. The bike was followed by several noisy and notorious 'bangers'.

Services were held in Ardross in Rev MacDonald and Rev Muirden's time, but Mr MacCallum can remember a special Congregation Meeting held there, which he and the Rev A Howe of the Church of Scotland, Alness attended. This was a meeting of the people of Ardross to decide the way forward with regard

to the services in Ardross Church. They then met with the trustees
of Ardross and decided upon an Open Day. Thereafter, services
were held most Sundays, Mr MacCallum taking approximately
one per month.

**Old And New Manses, And Other Financial Business**
It was in the MacCallums' time that the decision was taken to
sell the old manse and build a new one. The old manse was cold
and damp. Some of the rooms were not even in use. The manse
needed extensive renovation, having no central heating, damp
course etc., and there was no money to do this, so they decided
to sell. The new manse was built on part of the church's own glebe.

'During 1976 the old manse and glebe were sold, proceeds
going to provision of a new manse. We retained part of the glebe
on which the present manse is built. This site is the property of
the congregation, having purchased the glebe in 1921. The manse
was completed in July 1976 being built by Pat Munro Ltd, at a
cost of £23,296.00.

'The following year 1977 the repainting of the church was
undertaken. This was the first time since the church was opened
for public worship in 1900 that repainting was undertaken. The
work was done by Messrs H R McGregor, Dingwall, at a cost of
£3,602.00. At the same time a new water supply, carpeting and
vinyl was obtained at a further cost of £430.00.

'In 1978 our attention turned to the Alness Hall. The interior
of this hall was in poor state of repair, part of the ceiling having
fallen sometime previously, and it was necessary to renew the
ceiling. This was done at a cost of £634.00, then repainting of
the whole hall for £859.00 and completed by purchase of carpet
and vinyl for a further £274.00.

These are the main expenses on the buildings during the time
of Mr MacCallum's ministry from 1969 to 1979 totalling
£29,095.00.' Mr Roy Harmon (Treasurer)

**Sunday School**

Mrs MacKenzie takes up the story of the Sunday School, which had been meeting in the Alness Hall.

'A new problem arose: Alness and Invergordon are miles apart, and the Invergordon children needed transport to get to the Alness hall. Rev. Hugh MacCallum changed the arrangement. He reckoned that the best thing to do was to hold only one Sunday School in the church, during the morning service. This is the procedure we follow today. The Sunday School in the church began with only four pupils – Anne Marie and John MacKenzie and Norman and Rosemary MacAulay. From then on the number in the Sunday School has risen. The young people who leave the Bible Class usually go to the Youth Fellowship, and stay in the congregation.

'We are thankful for every single child we see in the Sunday School, but we can never be complacent about numbers or any other aspect of our work.

'As the Sunday School grew in size, accommodation became a problem. I began with the founding four in the lower vestry. Then we graduated to the upper one. On separate occasions, a class was taught on the stairs. During the tenure of Professor John L MacKay, the boiler room below ground level was brought into use, but we still didn't have the space we needed for teaching purposes.

'Exams, too, have been coped with by generations of Rosskeen children in surroundings that varied greatly. Early on, the venue was the old manse and Mr Muirden's big dining table. Then came the desks in Bridgend school. There followed a spell when drawing boards had to be balanced on church pews and the answers written there. Doing the exams in the basement was a big improvement, but was hampered by the limited space, lack of tables and proper lighting.'

One of the children who lived through these years is Colin David MacKenzie, who is still a worshipper with Rosskeen today:

'I remember quite vividly the day we went on our Sunday

School outing to Golspie and the bus broke down. By the time we arrived and after being presented with our certificates it was time to go home. Despite this, everybody enjoyed the day. During the month of January, we always had our winter party in the Alness Hall. All the children of the congregation would be enthralled by the games (pass the parcel – which I hated as I never won!). Many watched wide-eyed as sausage rolls, cakes, ice cream etc. would emerge from the small kitchen at the back. At the end of the day we would all go home with our presents and our bags of cakes, which was mostly eaten before we got home.

'The late 70s were a watershed for Rosskeen – a new manse was built and the church received a coat of paint after eighty years. Surprisingly, I liked the old manse – solid stone building, but cold, no central heating, except a large range/Rayburn in the kitchen.'

Rosemary Wilson (nee MacAulay) was one of the 'founding four':

'Rosskeen Sunday School in the early 70s was a very different place when compared with today. I used to go to Sunday School with my elder brother, Norman, and Anne-Marie and John MacKenzie. A few years later my brother John came too. This was the *whole* Sunday School.

'We were the only children from our school who went and this made us feel very "different" from our peers, which we did not like one bit.

'When we used to drive through Invergordon High Street on a Sunday, if either of us saw anyone we knew we used to shout "DUCK", and duck down and hide in the back of the car!

'Today it is so amazing to see God's work in the Sunday School (and in the congregation) when comparing the past with the present. My own children have many friends in the Sunday School and this makes it more enjoyable for them.

'Two things have not changed. One is the sound foundation of Biblical knowledge taught by those who willingly take on this difficult task – and do a fantastic job. The other is the constant provision of sweets by Mrs MacKenzie – which was always a great source of encouragement to us.'

## The Kilmuir Connection

Mrs Katy Ross reminds us that:

'Over the years, until it closed in 1978, the Kilmuir Easter Free Church played a significant role in the religious life of the area. At one time it served a wide and flourishing farming community. Latterly, changes in farming, mechanisation and other factors, meant that there were fewer people engaged on the land and churches suffered as a consequence. Kilmuir Easter Church was a fine building and was quite a landmark. Situated about five miles to the east of Rosskeen, they were very much sister churches.

'My memory goes back to 1952 (or 1954), when my husband, the late Rev. Donald Ross succeeded the late Rev. S MacIver as minister. From the beginning there was a close relationship and co-operation between the two churches. The late Rev. John Muirden was then the highly esteemed minister at Rosskeen, and the late John Bruce, along with George MacLeod and Kenny MacIver were assessor elders to Kilmuir Easter.

'Kilmuir Easter received great help and encouragement from the friends at Rosskeen, especially at communions, and other special occasions. Likewise, Kilmuir Easter supported Rosskeen and it was the custom to close Kilmuir Easter for the Rosskeen Communion services.

'My memories are of the many happy times of fellowship in both churches and their respective manses.

'There are few members of the Kilmuir Easter Church surviving today. One of the best known was Miss Kate Munro of Tullich, who died in 1996. Latterly, although unable to attend in person, she maintained a keen interest in all its affairs, watching the sermons on video tape. Those who knew her, spoke highly of her humble and gracious manner, and her hardy, independent spirit. She mourned the way the Lord's Day is not kept nowadays. In days gone by not a sound would break the peace, but now tractors fly around from dawn to dusk. Regardless of her own condition, she constantly testified that "the Almighty One has been good to me".

Her obituary in *The Ross-shire Journal*, makes interesting reading: 'On Sunday April 21, Catherine Fraser Munro, of Tullich Croft, Delny, died aged 93. Kate was a well loved crofting character of Tullich.

The highlight of her childhood summers were the days spent by the burn, tramping the blankets and the regretted playfulness with an over frisky lamb which caused her to land in the burn.

How she loved the deep chaff autumn mattress, but oh the itch by spring! Kate had her tonsils removed on the kitchen table and her 'lost' voice restored by being plugged into the galvanic battery.

In her fitter days she loved nothing better than the day trip to Oban and Fort William organised by the local district nurse.

Kate had happily ploughed and harrowed by horse, hated spreading lime by shovel and resignedly helped scythe a heavy, fallen oat crop and sheathed it by hand. Kate's life remained simple and uncluttered – to Kate a spade was a spade, as many of us knew to our cost!

A fiercely held wish of Kate's was that she would end her days in the home she grew up in. Very thankfully this was made possible by Alness and Invergordon Medical Group who had agreed to join a Scottish Office funded pilot scheme whereby 24 hour hospital service could be made available.

Kate very fittingly was the first patient to receive this care.

For the final week of Kate's life she was nursed at home by sensitive, caring and responsive professionals. This was a great comfort to Kate and all her friends. True to form Kate fought hard to the end, but died peacefully at home. Many thanks to all involved from all Kate's friends in Tullich.'

At one Kilmuir Easter Communion in Rev. Donald Ross's time, while the congregation duly kept singing verse after verse there was a bit of a commotion going on in the vestry. The two elders 'on duty' were Mr Kenny MacIver and Mr Davy MacLeod and they had a problem! There was a cork in the bottle of wine and they had nothing to remove it. No knife, no screwdriver, nothing! So the enterprising elders decided to break the neck of the bottle, which resulted in the trousers of Kenny's suit being splashed with the wine. Eventually they made their way into the church (probably much to the relief of the elders!).

Mrs Katy Ross continues:
'I believe that eternity alone will reveal the fruits of many years of humble, but devoted service of members, elders, ministers and indeed of many secret disciples who all belonged to the old church at Kilmuir Easter.'

In 1978, two years after the death of Rev. Donald Ross, it was finally decided to close Kilmuir Easter Free Church, but sacred memories will linger on in the hearts of those who now happily maintain their witness within the fellowship of Rosskeen Free Church.

At the time, Rev. Hugh MacCallum went round all the folks with any connection with Kilmuir Easter to ask how they felt about joining Rosskeen. He was Interim Moderator and had been a tower of strength in the interim period. It seemed fitting that the congregation should join with their friends in Rosskeen. The final service in Kilmuir Easter was conducted by Rev. Hugh MacCallum. It is interesting to note that young Donald MacGregor, grandson of Rev. Donald Ross, was baptised at this service. This family was firmly established in the worship and witness in Rosskeen, until they moved to live in Inverness in 1997, where they now worship at Smithton Free Church.

Morag MacGregor is a daughter of Rev. Donald and Mrs Katy Ross, and she along with her husband Roy are the parents of baby Donald mentioned above, and they now have three more boys. Morag also has fond memories of Kilmuir Easter church, where she grew up in the manse in Delny:

'Delny or Kilmuir Easter Free Church manse was an attractive country house set well off the main road and sheltered by a variety of tall trees and hedges. On the south it was bordered by a fast flowing burn, which provided a popular but dangerous play area for us. As far as the manse family was concerned it was an idyllic setting. On the one hand we enjoyed all the privacy and space of the manse and its environment, while on the other, it was readily accessible to such exciting amenities as MacLeod's shop at Barbaraville, and the Jackdaw Hotel, where Katherine and I worked our holidays.

'Having plenty of ground round the manse, it was natural for us to have livestock. This ranged from the most amazing collection of hens, one of which displayed a quite remarkably aggressive personality and was known to have chased more than one terrified visitor round the manse until they were thankfully rescued by an open door. There were cats and dogs, too, of many strange breeds and temperaments. Often they were rejects from other people's homes because at Delny manse there seemed to be room for all sorts of animals and humans. The "ever open door" as Granny MacKinnon was often heard to say.

'Horses were also very much part of the scene and it was not uncommon for unsuspecting guests to scream out in terror as one over-friendly horse called Paddy would walk boldly through the front door and into the drawing room to greet everyone there!

'One of the most exciting things about growing up in Delny manse was the wonderful variety of relations – cousins, uncles and aunts who all came back and fore regularly to stay or visit. The manse was never locked, at least not securely, and so it was quite usual to come home from school to find visitors drinking tea in the warm kitchen, where the kettle was always boiling on the Rayburn. Mum and Dad would appear later.

'You will gather that life in Delny manse was a happy and

exciting experience for children – but it was a Free Church manse
and this made it very special for Katherine, Angus and myself.
It provided the freedom, security, fun and laughter of a good
home where we were surrounded by loving parents. Within this
freedom there was also the very strong firm discipline and
restraints of Christian living. As young children we took this for
granted, but as we grew into our teenage years, we naturally
began to question the strict rules and regulations which governed
our lives. There was daily family worship, when often we would
have preferred to be doing our own thing. There were strict rules
about Sunday – no television, no walks past the gates, no playing
with friends and no bicycle or horse rides. Generally Sunday
was a very solemn day – morning and afternoon services, with
Sunday School in between and at communion times it seemed
to be services all day, ending up with long worship before
"escaping" to bed. The only real relief was when visiting
adventurous cousins kept less rigidly to the Sunday rules. We
supported them to the hilt and did things which would not have
been approved of by our long-suffering parents.

    'I remember one of those forbidden adventures involved
climbing out of my bedroom window and heading for a disco in
Tain. My parents, in blissful ignorance of my whereabouts,
thought I was in bed early with toothache. My brother Angus
was persuaded to warn anyone from disturbing me. After dancing
the night away until about 2 o'clock in the morning, myself and
my friends hitched a lift home. We were one of the first cars to
arrive at the scene of a tragic accident where five teenagers from
Alness were hit and killed by a car. They had just left the disco in
front of us. I must say, I was taught a lesson that night. I could have
been one of those walking home – my parents not even knowing
I was out. That was the last time I escaped out of the window.

    'Growing up in a Free Church manse was restricting at times
to a strong-willed teenager, but looking back, it was certainly a
privilege and an enriching experience. Most important, was the
influence for good which it brought to bear on our lives in later

years. I shall always remember those years of my childhood and youth with deep gratitude.'

**Report From Mr Roy Harmon, Treasurer**

When the congregation at Kilmuir Easter became vacant with the death of Rev. Donald Ross, the Presbytery of Tain appointed Rev. Hugh MacCallum as Interim Moderator. This was a small congregation, who were mainly advanced in years. I understand services were discontinued in 1978, and in 1979 the congregation agreed to apply for consolidation with Rosskeen. This was agreed and granted at the Assembly of 1980. The buildings of the Kilmuir Easter congregation, i.e. church and manse at Kilmuir and church at Logie were considered to be surplus to requirements for the new congregation. The Assembly of 1980 granted permission for church and manse at Kilmuir to be sold, the proceeds to be lodged with the General Trustees on behalf of the Congregation and Church Extension Committee with certain conditions. These buildings were sold in 1981 and settlement reached in 1982. This amount was known as Kilmuir Easter Manse Fund and under terms of Finding of Assembly in 1980 we were able to reclaim same to assist in purchase of 'The Nurseries' in 1990. 'The Nurseries', Saltburn, is now the manse of Rosskeen's Assistant Minister. Regarding Logie Easter Church building – the Kilmuir Easter session had petitioned 1977 General Assembly for permission to sell as it was no longer in use. This was granted with condition that 'net amount' received be lodged with General Trustees, income from same being utilised for congregational purposes. This building was unsold at the time of Consolidation but was sold in 1982.

Some statistics from Mr MacCallum's ministry

|  | MARRIAGES | BAPTISMS | DEATHS |
|---|---|---|---|
| ROSSKEEN | 12 | 36 | 50 |
| ARDROSS | 4 | 4 | 0 |
| DELNY | 0 | 1 | 0 |

## Margaret's Story

'Nearly twenty years ago on a Sunday morning I sat in Rosskeen Free Church just as I had done previously for many a Sunday – but this Sunday was an extra special one for me as it was the day I first came to know our Lord. I listened intently to the words preached by Rev. Hugh MacCallum and felt that in my heart every spoken word came from our Lord and it was especially for me. I cannot find the words to express the change that came into my life from then onwards.

'Rev. Hugh MacCallum told me about a post that was about to appear in the Monthly Record as a Matron for senior girls in Hebron School in South India. I applied for the post and soon found myself in this vast sub-continent – it was like being in another world and a great and wonderful experience for me. I can never thank our Lord enough for taking me to India and can only count it a great privilege in doing anything for our Lord, He who has done everything for me.

'I was only 49 years old when I went to India, had never been out of Britain and had never flown. I went from Inverness – London – Bombay – Bangalore – Combatyore. After a three hour journey in an old ambassador taxi to a place called Ootacamund, over 12,000 feet up in the Nilgari Hills, I must admit I was physically tired , but I arrived safe and sound with all my luggage intact. Oh the marvellous care our Lord had taken of me and guided my every footstep. I love India and its people. A few months before I left India, we at Hebron School had heard of Alison MacDonald's disappearance. A young student who had gone to India with a friend for a holiday, so many prayers were said for her safe return. We can only keep on praying and wherever Alison is, may our Lord be with her.'

Mrs Margaret Plenderleith (nee MacLennan)

## Hugh's Story

'As I begin to write this, I have just come back from a weekend break in Nairn. Whilst worshipping in Nairn Free Church, one of their elders remarked that the Rosskeen congregation gave him hope for the work in Nairn. His optimism arises from the fact that while living in Easter Ross he remembers how small our congregation was then. Under the ministry of the Rev. Hugh MacCallum (1969-79) the congregation saw an encouraging growth, both numerically and spiritually, with a distinct interest in the gospel evidenced. As I look back I can now see that the Spirit was at work in the church.

'In 1978 I was aware of a dissatisfaction in my life but I didn't have the sense to realise that its source was spiritual; in spite of all that I had heard and had been taught since childhood. At the November '78 Communion, my brother Murdo made a profession of his faith for the first time which was to be used by God to make me realise that my real need was Jesus. Murdo had been converted earlier in the year but his conversion didn't awaken me to my own spiritual need. Having been brought up in the Free Church I knew that the public profession that Murdo was making was a solemn act – something not to be undertaken lightly. Looking back I can see that the Lord used Murdo's profession to make me attentive and receptive that day.

'The minister taking that particular service was the late Rev. John MacLeod of Gairloch. I can't remember his text, nor the content of his sermon, but while speaking at the Lord's table he pointed out that two professions were being made that day. Those at the Lord's table were saying they were the Lord's and those sitting away were saying they were not. This was the very arrow which struck home and made me realise that my need was Jesus. That day a spiritual battle began within my heart, with the old nature fighting back resolutely to keep me from yielding in prayer, to Jesus. My thoughts were confused and two sleepless nights followed. Thankfully the Lord continued to strive with me and eventually broke my resistance, causing me to kneel at the side of my bed, in prayer to him. On reflection, the days that followed were days of joy and peace in believing, until I was made to realise that this old nature still had plenty of fight left –

even in its death throes. I am very thankful for my upbringing – for the teaching received at home, in the church, and in the Sunday School. This gave me a good grounding and definitely helped me later. I also derived great benefit and real blessing from other Christians – Lindsay MacCallum in particular was a great help.

'In the environment in which I was brought up, I had just accepted God's existence, but early in 1979 I experienced a period of doubt about God. Thankfully this was short but it was filled with dark thoughts and feelings within, which were difficult to share. God, however, lifted these thoughts through the reading of His own word – from Romans chapter 10. What a load was lifted from me that day!

'On pondering over the years since my conversion, I am amazed at God's patience with me and thankful that he is the God of grace and mercy.' (Hugh MacIver)

### Mrs Jessie MacKenzie on Rev Hugh MacCallum

'The first time we ever met Mr. MacCallum was the first Sunday after we arrived from Glasgow in 1974. There was a baptism that Sunday, only later did we find out it was his twin grandchildren, Pamella and Patricia Black. The following week Mr MacCallum visited us, Unfortunately when my young son opened the door to our first visitor, he shut the door on the poor man. Fortunately, he saw the funny side of it.

'We got to know Mr and Mrs MacCallum very well as both were from our own part of the world – Kilchoan, Skye and Glasgow – and knew people that David and I knew well. Mr MacCallum being previously a joiner and David a carpenter, they had a lot in common.

'The following years we got to know both of them very well, in times of family bereavements, good news, illness, unemployment etc., and they were always there when we needed them. At the end of 1978 David was made redundant. The only offer of a job was in Rosyth. We were feeling very sad, as we were very happy here, and thought we would need to move again.

Rev. MacCallum came to visit us and prayed that David would get a job locally. The following week we got a phone call offering him his previous job back. That was in 1978 and David is still in the same job, twenty years later. This shows the power of prayer.

'In 1983 when I was very ill in Raigmore Hospital, Mr MacCallum was one of five ministers who visited me. His visit not only cheered me up, but everyone else in the ward too. He had a chat with everyone in the ward (in these days it was the old hospital, with big long wards). Before he left, everyone who was able to get up, gathered round my bed and he prayed for us all. They were from all denominations.

'It was during Mr MacCallum's ministry that we had the shortest Sunday service ever. One of the elders forgot the keys so we had the service outside, which lasted about five minutes as it was snowing. Colin was very happy as he had got home early!! We were always made very welcome in the manse, even while picking brambles and arriving in wellies and old clothes!

'We were very sorry when he got the call to Kilchoan in1979 but we wished him well. Members of the congregation, including my mother and I travelled to Kilchoan by bus for his Induction, which was a memorable day. It is nice that when he retired he returned to Alness and is now among us all again in Rosskeen.'

Mr MacCallum received and accepted a call from Kilchoan Free Church in October 1979, having served at Rosskeen for nine years and eleven months. Both he and Mrs MacCallum were very sad to leave and they missed Rosskeen more than they had expected.

Living in Kilchoan meant they saw more of their son Aeneas, his wife Sandra and their family. This proved to be providential, as, in August of 1980, Aeneas died very suddenly, aged thirty-four.

Mr MacCallum retired from Kilchoan in 1981, and moved to Caol, where they stayed until December 1992. Mrs MacCallum had by now suffered two strokes and their son Kenny had been diagnosed as having terminal cancer. They moved back to Alness to be nearer to their daughter, Mary Black, who lives there with her husband Ian. Kenny died on 20th December 1982, just as they were flitting to 8 Kendal Crescent, where he now lives alone, his wife having died on 26th March 1988.

On Friday, 18th November 1994, a company of members and friends of Rosskeen and friends from Kiltearn met to celebrate Mr. Hugh MacCallum's twenty-five years in the Ministry. An invitation had been sent to the congregation at Kilchoan, but they were unable to attend.

After a lovely tea provided by the ladies of the Afternoon Fellowship Committee, Rev. Kenny MacDonald very ably chaired the proceedings. Until that point, Mr. MacCallum was the only one in the room not to realise why we were gathered together. His daughter, Mary, brought in a cake which he duly cut. Kenny spoke lovingly of Mr. MacCallum's service for the Lord in his ministry. Davie MacLeod presented a Bible on behalf of his many friends. Willie MacKenzie spoke on behalf of the folks from other congregations and Mr MacCallum, in his own gracious way, replied.

After a psalm led by Davie MacLeod, Mr MacCallum closed a lovely afternoon with prayer.

We as a congregation are richly blessed in that Mr. MacCallum continues to worship with us in Rosskeen. We are thankful for his good health, his words of comfort and understanding to those who are suffering, for his gentle and gracious nature, for his wisdom regarding adverse weather (' It is better than we deserve!') and for his excellent pots of broth at Communion time! He is always ready to take a Prayer Meeting or service at short notice, and is much in demand as a guest preacher in other congregations. The reverence, gratitude and praise for the Almighty, which characterise his prayers are a great testimony from a humble and godly man who has known much personal sorrow in his lifetime. We are thankful to God for the privilege of his fellowship.

# CHAPTER 5

# REV JOHN L MACKAY

In October 1979 Mr MacCallum left to take up his new charge in his native Ardnamurachan. The Reverend John L. MacKay came to Rosskeen after completing his studies in the Free Church College. He was ordained and inducted on 8th February 1980, and the reception took place in Bridgend School, Alness.

He was born and educated in Glasgow, and graduated from Glasgow University with an MA in 1970. In 1973 he gained a M.Litt at Oxford University, and then a BD from London University in 1979.

John Mackay's induction at the beginning of the 1980s heralded the beginning of a new era and a new style of preaching. Mr. Mackay was a very able preacher and teacher, and with his strong, powerful voice, he demanded the attention of the congregation. Donald Stirling recalls: 'To speak about the exactness of John Mackay's preaching in no way takes away from Rev. Hugh MacCallum at all. The latter's preaching style was "homely", talking plainly to people, which certainly had an effect on my life. I do remember my soul beginning to be stirred under his preaching, but with John MacKay you could see the "lecturer" style – exact and precise. It was very much a teaching ministry.'

Hugh Ferrier recounts some of Professor MacKay's gifts as a person and minister: 'John is a very private, shy and unassuming person with very high principles. The only information he would let his mother divulge to me is the above dates and details of his academic qualifications.

'He is also a practical man. The first time I met John was in May 1978, when he was a student. He was taxi driver to my father in the year he was Moderator. He was a very good taxi driver!

'John is very honest and direct. At the first election of deacons when I was in Rosskeen, he came to the house to tell me that my name would not be put forward for the office of deacon, as I was not very regular at attending prayer meetings. I know that this must have been very difficult for him – but John would never avoid what he saw to be his duty.

'John is very Christ-centred and outreach minded. When I came to Rosskeen in August 1981, after getting the job of Chemistry and Maths teacher at Invergordon Academy, John was the new minister and there was a definite 'buzz' in the church. The outreach work had started with a Sunday school in Milnafua. Quite a few people became members, including myself (by disjunction certificate).

'John is also a very original and thoroughly prepared preacher. He thinks down lines of thought, which are unusual, novel and thought provoking. One amazing sermon he preached was titled 'Whatever happened to the dinosaurs?' He postulated that man and the dinosaurs co-existed and that 'leviathan' is a better description of a dinosaur than the usually accepted crocodile.

'Finally, John is steeped in the Bible, and has what seems to me an encyclopaedic knowledge of it. In my first year of teaching, I had visits from Jehovah's Witnesses at both my parents' home in Inverness and at my house in Invergordon. My view of the Trinity took a severe shaking. Without knowing about this, John came for a visit, and then went through Paul's writings from his head, giving evidence for the Trinity.

'These are just a few memories of John's character, which come to mind. They are not in chronological order and maybe not in order of importance. I have the greatest of respect and affection for him, and look back on the short time I enjoyed his ministry as a great privilege.'

James Campbell writes that: 'John MacKay's gifts were made manifest in his preaching and teaching the word of God. He would occupy the pulpit, tall and erect with his head raised, and with a confidence (not a total self-confidence which comes as a result of man's pride), but a confidence attributed firstly to his own intellect and a clear mind, secondly to having thoroughly prepared his text and his sermon. The third (and the most important aspect of his ministry) was godliness. John MacKay was, and I believe still is, a man whose whole confidence is in God himself, and this showed itself in his ministry, in his preaching and in his prayers. In his preaching and in his prayers he desired nothing more than the glory of God.

'John L. very often would preach from a text which is fairly familiar, and used by many other preachers previously. I would say to myself, 'Well, I have a fairly good idea what's coming here' and I was always wrong, for he would take from a text so much that you would not think of. I remember a series of sermons on the 'Sermon on the Mount' and how he expounded the 'Beatitudes'. What a privilege to sit under this man's preaching.

'The sermons that stick in my mind most of all, not that I can remember them in much detail, are those preached on Genesis. I remember particularly one preached on a Sunday evening in the hall at Perrins Road in Alness. He was preaching on the flood, and I remember how he caught our attention and particularly that of the young people, when he stopped speaking for a moment, and then presented the question, "Whatever happened to the dinosaurs?". He went on to give a vivid description of the flood, and how it was a geological disaster on the world. Not only did it rain, but there was this tremendous upheaval as the waters came up from the deep causing devastation on the earth, resulting in the fossilisation of what lived on the earth at the time of the flood. His preaching gave you a confidence in the account of creation and the flood, as we have it in the Word of God.

'Some years later in 1987 he was invited back to Rosskeen to open the new Church hall at Achnagarron, and at the weekend he was asked to give a talk or lecture on creation. There again he was extremely well prepared. "Evolution", he said, "is not a science, it is only dressed up as a science. Nobody was around when the world was created, there was no one there to take records and evaluations, Evolution is a theory."

'John MacKay helped much in different ways in the Deacons' Court. He was especially helpful when it came to legal affairs. It would not be proper to mention anything specific, but when he dealt with any business it was carried out thoroughly, and there would be no come back in an eventuality.

'Disciples of the gospel of Jesus Christ are called from many different walks of life. Jesus called those who were fishermen and tax collectors to be his disciples, and the apostle Paul, who was a Pharisee, was dramatically called by the Lord Jesus himself. Never in his wildest dreams would Paul have thought of himself as a 'servant of Jesus Christ', and God today is still changing people's lives and very often redirecting them as his servants and into full time service. Some may have been teachers, plumbers, doctors or even joiners!

'When John MacKay came to Rosskeen, I was an adherent in the church, and I used to enjoy a snooze in the back seat. I was brought by the preaching of the Word of God to see my own need and my sin. I became a member in Rosskeen Free Church in 1981 and it was a privilege to sit under John L's preaching and to serve with him in the Deacons' Court.'

Hugh MacIver recalls that John MacKay, in his first year, had to take two funerals from the MacIver family. "The first was Kenny and Peggy's son Richard, who died at birth, and then Dad's (Kenny MacIver, Senior). It was on the day that Dad died that a small incident happened, for which I hold him in high regard.

'As we were hustling and bustling about doing things (obeying sisters, as brothers tend to do), there was John sitting beside mam, holding her hand to comfort her. This was more than I expected him to do.

'His preaching was his strong point for me as a young Christian. It was good to be under such a ministry to help me grow. His confidence in God's Word being true shone through.

'I remember his first sermon was on "Being justified by faith"

– the foundational teaching of the Reformed Church. We were a well taught people.

'I particularly remember three of his sermons which helped me: The two preached after my father's death: "Let me die the death of the righteous and let my last end be like his" (Num. 23 :10); "The Lord knoweth them that are his" (2 Tim. 2:19). The third, I can remember neither time nor text, but it was a Sunday evening in the Alness Hall. I had spent a wearying afternoon discussing spiritual matters with Jehovah's Witnesses at my door. All the fiery darts of the devil were put out as John MacKay preached on Christ's Deity.

'John MacKay's time with us at Rosskeen was well spent. I, as a fairly young Christian, certainly benefitted from it, and was sad to see him go. But I know God has given him the gifts to more than ably fill the position he now holds.'

Donald Stirling remembers: 'My wife, Janice and I arrived up in Alness in July 1976, and three weeks later Kevin was born. Hugh MacCallum baptised Kevin in October 1976 and Mark in July 1979. It was during Hugh's ministry that I began seeking. Full of my Church of Scotland upbringing, I really struggled with the psalm singing and the type of service at Rosskeen, but gradually these issues faded as the Spirit began to work in me.

'My first impression of Rosskeen was meeting Davie MacLeod, who saw me arrive and was instantly halfway down the front steps with his hand outstretched in welcome. He was so gracious.

'By the end of the MacCallum ministry I was a very earnest seeker. All my preconceived ideas were slowly but surely being changed. By the time John MacKay came with his teaching and application I was "ripe for harvest". I was drinking in the gospel. I can remember badgering Hugh MacIver and Lindsay MacCallum about gospel truths. Sometimes I heard Christian jargon I didn't understand, but I just clung on because I wanted to know more and more.

'In November 1980 Rev John MacCallum came to preach at

the Communion. That was the one where I knew that I had given my life to Christ. The preacher spoke about the Cross in very graphic detail – the pain, the blood, the cost. He left us in no doubt about how painful and cruel was Christ's death on the Cross. When it came to the time when the members went forward, I had to physically pin myself to the seat to stop me joining them. I wanted to go to the Lord's Table, but this was the Free Church, and the formalities had not been observed – I hadn't been to a Session, I didn't have a token, I didn't know what to do. So I sat, and looked on, and knew I should have been at the Table. My decision was made.

'The next Communion was in February 1981. It was the first one taken by John MacKay, and as far as my memory goes, I think I was the only new member. The Saturday night preparation service was in the Alness Hall and I stayed back for the Session. The next day I took my place as one of the Lord's people at his Table, remembering his death, till he returns.

'What I remember most about John MacKay was his exactness. Every sermon had every 't' crossed and every 'I' dotted. He had the ability to make you sit up and take notice. He chose subjects that I had never heard anyone else preach on. The one that stands out most is, 'Whatever happened to the dinosaurs'!

'At that particular time I was really into the Creation v Evolution debate. I was reading up about it, and here, one Sunday evening, John MacKay just waded straight in. It was compelling preaching – full attention required! I'm afraid I've forgotten the full structure of the sermon, but basically he traced the dinosaurs from Creation to the flood, and how we read about the last of them in Job 40 and 41 – the Behemoth and the Leviathan. (I wish I had a copy of that tape.)

'The other sermon that really had me totally focused was the Christmas Story, centred around the Wise Men. Now this particular morning I was very alert, almost as if the Holy Spirit was preparing me for a sermon that I have often since quoted, as it made such an impact on me.

'John MacKay began by listing all the misconceptions the world has about this time. He told us that the "Magi" (Wise Men/Kings) never saw Christ in the manger. He took us back to Leviticus 12, giving the time scale for purification following birth that a woman was required to adhere to in those days, before being allowed to enter the Temple. The detail was given regarding the sacrifices which were required, and then referring to Luke 2:24, he showed that the actual sacrifice offered was a humble one (a pair of doves) – that of a person who could not afford even a lamb, and certainly no gold or precious things, indicating that at this point, the family were very poor. If the Wise Men had visited the manger, Mary and Joseph would have been able to offer a greater sacrifice, because of the Wise Men's gifts.

'Finally, he took us to Matthew 2:11, and the Magi visiting Jesus in "the house". To me, this was tremendous – we had been taken through a detailed study of the Bible, to a place of more knowledge, understanding and excitement about the Bible, our Saviour's beginnings in this world.'

Donald's wife Janice explains how her husband's decision to make a public confession of faith in Christ had a powerful effect upon her own spiritual state.

'There were quite a number of converts during the three years John MacKay was our minister. Maybe we were all 'ripe for the harvest', but there can be no doubt that he was thorough in proclaiming the gospel. One sermon in particular was about the reality of hell. I was not converted at the time. He spoke of the need to hear and realise that hell was what awaits those who do not respond to Christ's call to come to him. He referred to us leaving church out through the front doors as though they were the gates of hell, if we heard and did not respond. That was powerful.

'I was earnestly seeking when Donald went forward in the February. The children were young and so were at home, so it was only Donald and I in the pew. We were sitting very near the Communion Tables. The two middle tables were set, and the call was given for the members to go down. Donald got up and left me *alone* in the pew. The separation had taken place – Donald was with the Lord's people, I was not. That was powerful.

'After the service, as is the nature of us all, we were blethering outside church, and I very soon realised the small group I was in were all chatting about the service and the lovely Communion, and I was desolate. In that small group, I was the only unconverted person. That was powerfully used to make me see I was really not just the "outsider", but that I was OUTSIDE OF CHRIST.

'By November of that year, I had to stop fighting and give in to the pull of the gospel. There was no "Damascus Road", just a constant growing realisation that Christ was the missing part of my life. I now knew I needed him for every part of my life. The fight was over, and the Christian "battle" begun. I went forward for the first time at the November '81 Communion, which was taken by Rev Calum Lamont of Plockton and Kyle (now retired). (Mr Lamont was by this time, the father-in-law of John MacKay).'

## Outreach in Milnafua

'It was in John MacKay's time that the Sunday School in Milnafua was started. The Session decided that the church ought to be engaged in outreach, and where better to start than in the housing scheme nearest the church.

'The plan was that there would be a time of praying about the matter in personal prayer and also as a congregation in a special prayer time after the midweek meeting to ask the Lord's blessing on the outreach and the plans. There was tremendous prayer back-up. On Sunday evenings we met in David and Anne Wilkie's home for talk, planning and prayer. This was the fact: the work in Milnafua was rooted and grounded in prayer.

'The first 'door-to-door' was on a wet Saturday in September '81, and the Lord's answering of prayer was obvious. We arrived at the car park and prayed in our cars for the Lord to bless and for the rain to stop. We got out of our cars and the rain stopped. We went round the doors, finished, and got back into our cars and the rain began again! This happened twice!

'As for knocking on the doors, it was obvious that the Holy Spirit had been there before us. We experienced no opposition – in fact, we were given a warm welcome 99% of the time – the most negative reception being a "No thank you".

'Although the main aim of the outreach was to find out what interest there was among the adults and to invite them out to church, it soon became obvious that the need was for the children. Although the adults were interested, they were not committing themselves, but were very eager that their children should go, and asked if there was a Sunday School.

'This sent us back to the praying and thinking stage, and more meetings at the Wilkies' in Invergordon, of which the outcome was that we would set up a Sunday School in the Community Hall in Milnafua (as transporting the children to and from the church would have been a problem).

'I remember the first day of the Sunday School – I was inside setting up chairs and tables, and as the start-time arrived, there were no children. On asking Angela MacDonald, "Are there any children in sight?", she replied: "Yes, Lindsay is talking to them at the door." So I thought, "Och well, there are one or two, that's not so bad", *then* , about forty children came rushing through the door!

'At first, the Sunday School met at 3pm, but eventually it was changed to 10.30am. Lindsay MacCallum was the first superintendent. The teachers were his sister Angela MacDonald, Murdo MacIver, Anne Ferrier and Donald Stirling.

'I really enjoyed my time in the Sunday School there and it was as much a learning experience for me as for the children, especially those from primary six to secondary age, as they were introduced to Christian summer camps and our own Sunday School outings, which we should continue to pray will yet reap a harvest in their lives.' (Donald & Janice Stirling)

John MacKay moved into the manse as a bachelor, and as the congregation became more familiar with the young man, it was assumed that, given his shy personality and reservedness, a bachelor he would stay. Nevertheless, as time went by, there was an attractive young lady in the congregation by the name of Mary who won the heart of the man, and what a surprise for the congregation as they read the announcement of their engagement in the *Press & Journal*. They were married in October 1980 and their first baby, also called John, was born in January 1982. Mary is a daughter of the Rev and Mrs Calum Lamont Plockton & Kyle.

Mary was an excellent lady of the manse. She had been a teacher at Bridgend Primary School in Alness, and brought her skills to her new roles. She started the Ladies Meetings and the Youth Fellowship.

The Ladies Bible Study began around this time too, under guidance of Marie MacKenzie and Chrissie MacAulay.

'In 1982, being a fairly recent incomer to Rosskeen, I was missing the fellowship of a Ladies' Bible Study, which I had enjoyed in my previous place of residence.

'Very casually, I mentioned this to a friend from Inverness as we travelled together. Very little time from this conversation had elapsed when I received a telephone call in which the caller said that she understood I wanted to start a Bible Study in Rosskeen! I was absolutely shocked and my immediate reaction was that that was not for me. However, it kept coming at me and I began to give it more serious thought. My next worry was whether this would be acceptable to the Rev MacKay. I need not have worried as he gave it full approval. Rather than having the full responsibility, I made contact with a friend and asked her if she would share the running of it with me. This she was very happy and willing to do so we decided to have it fortnightly and in alternate venues, her house one fortnight and mine the other. We then contacted a number of ladies explaining what we were thinking of and they were more than willing to join in with us.

'After some time, the numbers grew and we had to go our separate ways, one Bible Study in Alness and one in Invergordon. As time went on, more and more Bible Studies were commenced and now there is an average of five going on.' (Marie Mackenzie)

'The Bible Study was a new venture – it was definitely the right time for it. For myself, I had never been to a Bible Study before, and found it was a tremendous asset. Both ladies were well prepared, and their homes open and hospitable. We all have fond memories of these studies. The first one was the study of Ruth and Esther.' (Janice Stirling)

In April 1980 at the age of five years Richard Stirling began Sunday School for the first time. Unfortunately, this also coincided with the first day of the new speaker system which had been installed in the Church. Rev John L MacKay had a very strong voice anyway, and as he stepped up to the microphone to begin the service, it seemed to be all NOISE. Richard began to cry and could not be consoled. In those days Mums and Dads didn't leave their pews, so there were agitated parents, and a very distressed Richard, and a very loud voice!! Hankies were passed around to mop up the flood of tears!

Also in 1980, the Tape Ministry started, and John MacKay's tapes were enjoyed by many outside the congregation.

'In 1982, to meet the demand for more accommodation for the Sabbath School, the old boiler house at the rear of the church was converted into a room for the use of the Sabbath School. The work was carried out by James Campbell and George MacLeod.

'During 1982, as an Outreach Project, a service in Invergordon (South Lodge School) which had been in abeyance for a number of years was recommenced.

'Further to assist the work of the congregation, in July 1982, an election for new deacons was held. It was conducted in John MacKay's very ordered and precise way. James Campbell, Hugh MacIver, Murdo MacIver, Donald Stirling and the late Simon Allison were elected to serve.

'The main concern during late 1982 and early 1983 for the maintenance of the church property was the condition of the church windows. This was a large task for a small congregation, but we were enabled to prepare and protect all the windows. James Campbell again carried out all the work.' (Mr Roy Harmon, Treasurer)

### Aileen's Story

I'll never forget the first time I went to Rosskeen Free Church. Various things had happened to me to make me decide I was never going back to the church I had attended; after all I was thirteen – grown up in my outlook on life! (Oh to be wise…)

'My mother (she who is wise) was friendly with Chrissie MacAulay and suggested that I went to church with her instead.

'I remember walking to Callum and Chrissie's, not really up nor down about going to Rosskeen. I'm a bit of a music fan and car freak so I was looking forward to a bit of Beethoven and the drive in the Daimler.

'When the door was opened to the main part of the church I remember the atmosphere being fresh, airy and inviting. On reflection this was the Holy Spirit but at the time I just felt comfortable.

'The quiet of the place added to my comfort and when the late Davie MacLeod opened the door leading to the pulpit he immediately reminded me of my grandpa. Rev John L. MacKay looked pretty fierce in his black tie and white shirt but I remember thinking that he had kind eyes.

'I enjoy singing and was delighted to find the first psalm had a tune I recognised. By verse two (with Chrissie's reassuring smiles) I began to "sing up". Why don't they issue new people with a note which says:

"Don't worry about standing or sitting; the preacher will tell you what to do. But please remember, when singing, that any word ending in 'ed' should have a syllable and note of its own e.g. water-ed?" Another reassuring smile from Chrissie helped me get over my embarrassment!

'The sermon was clear, simple; yet left me wanting to know more. He spoke from the Bible and rarely used an illustration. I knew he believed what he said and was concerned for the people because not only did his eyes light up but his red cheeks went on fire, too!

'My life was never the same again. Rev John MacKay was not and is not a 'super human', nor is he to be worshipped. But he is a servant of God who helped me to understand the Bible better. Both he and his wife opened the manse to the few of us who were teenagers at the time and although I didn't particularly fancy a Friday night at the manse (what was I going to say to my mates?!), once again the Mackays were kind, caring and actually interested in me.

'When he stood in the pulpit and said that he was leaving to go to the College, although still not a professing Christian, I was gutted. He'd opened up God's Word to me by showing its relevancy to my life and I felt like he was leaving me part way through a book. However, I learned pretty soon after that, that it is God who changes people, not men (or even women).

'After various men preaching "with a view to a call" the congregation decided on a certain Kenny MacDonald. And the rest, as they say, is history....' (Aileen Mackay).

In 1983 at the Free Church of Scotland General Assembly, the Reverend John L. MacKay, minister of Rosskeen Free Church, was unanimously elected to serve in the Free Church College in Edinburgh as Professor of Hebrew and Old Testament Literature. Three years previously he had been a student there, now he was a professor. He left Rosskeen in August of that year.

John L Mackay is a noted preacher and teacher throughout the country and beyond. On the back cover of one of his books it says this of him: 'John L. MacKay is an internationally respected Old Testament scholar and is also in demand for conferences where his skill in the practical exposition and application of doctrine are well respected.'

It was the Rosskeen Free Church congregation's privilege to have had him first.

# CHAPTER 6

# REV KENNETH MACDONALD

Rev Kenneth MacDonald and his wife Reta came to Rosskeen in 1984. Reta is a native of Orkney and Kenny grew up on a croft on Skye – one of a big happy family of ten children. Kenny's aptitude for practical jokes began in early childhood, when he got up to various nonsenses like putting the primary school clock forward by three quarters of an hour so that everyone got home early. These skills have stood him in good stead in his pastoral duties!

As a Customs Officer in London, and then in Lewis where the couple raised their family of four on a croft, Kenny had the opportunities to meet many people from all nationalities. Kenny's desire to enter the ministry grew out of a love for the people he came into contact with, 'I had so many lovely friends who were tremendous people and yet they were going on from day to day without any knowledge of the Lord, without any knowledge that one day everything was going to come to an end.'

This growing desire to tell people about the Lord Jesus Christ led to him giving up the security of his job for the frugal and precarious existence of a trainee minister. Another contributory factor in this decision was an experience of his daughter Alison back in 1975: she became a committed Christian at a summer camp. Later she wrote to a friend: 'I feel I won't know what to do with my life unless the Lord takes me to India.'[1]

---

1. Used with permission from 'Alison – A Father's Search For His Missing Daughter' by Quentin MacFarlane, Mainstream Publishing.

## Alison

As things transpired, Kenny and Reta were living in Edinburgh in 1981 (he was studying to be a minister at the Free Church College) when Alison went missing – in India. On holiday with her university friend, Elizabeth Merry, Alison went for a walk one morning, and disappeared from a busy street, apparently without any witnesses to see what happened to her. Suddenly, their lives were turned upside-down. Over the next hours, Kenny was miraculously provided with money, visa, plane tickets and letters of introduction to contacts in high places.

Kenny describes the heartbreak of the next few days, as a massive search was mounted in the area surrounding the village of Sonamarg, to look for Alison's body. In his diaries, Kenny had written things like: 'Lord, I need you. Where are you?' His prayers weren't going anywhere – he was up against a solid wall. He sensed that God was not there for him – an alien experience for someone who normally has a close walk with the Lord. At this time of trouble, when he needed the Lord, he was not there for him. What was God saying to Kenny at this time? It wasn't until about a fortnight later, after a totally fruitless search, that Kenny suddenly thought: 'Alison is alive somewhere around here.' And it was then that the Lord came back into his life. It was as if he said: 'Well, you have made up your own mind that she is dead. You haven't referred to me. You are going about in your own little world of darkness. I'll wait till you come out. And it was when I started to think positively about Alison that the Lord came into my life much more.'

Kenny says, 'The Lord's hand has been with us through all this. Looking back you can see there were times when you should have collapsed with disappointment. One time I was so sure that I was within minutes of finding her, I was actually quivering, but nothing came of it.

'I don't ask, "Why us?" in any bitter way. I am intrigued. Deep down in my heart I am quite excited because I know the end result is going to be good. It is going to be amazing and it is an excitement that an ordinary family like ours should be used in a way that is beyond our own thoughts, beyond what we say or do.

'It has made us stronger people and has had an effect on other people worldwide. People have found the Lord again, and lifestyles have been changed after reading Alison's story. People who were well on the way to suicide have been brought back. It's too amazing just to write it all off.

'In a way it is beyond understanding because thousands of girls go missing. So why should this little girl, why should Alison still capture interest after nineteen years? But she does.'

Those who have not seen the 'loveliness of Christ' (to use a phrase of Kenny's) find such faith hard to understand. Ruth Wishart, writing in the *Scotsman* (14 May 1994) tells of her frustration that 'two transparently decent, caring people should choose to prolong their agony by persisting in the belief that Alison is still alive'. Yet she also records her 'sense of wonder, tinged with envy, at a brand of faith which offers them such certainty in the midst of such pain'.

## Rosskeen

In the final year of study at the Free Church College, students are required to preach in different churches. On the first of these preaching engagements, Kenny preached at Rosskeen, followed by other sermons all over the country. As the year went on, he was away nearly every Sunday and had completely forgotten Rosskeen to the extent that when, out of the blue, he received a unanimous call from Rosskeen congregation, he could hardly remember which church it was. He remembered the high pulpit, and the very small congregation who all sat hugging the back wall! At night he preached in the wee hall in Alness, which he really enjoyed. He knew Anne Ferrier quite well, and spent the afternoon at her house. Referring to the fact that another congregation had also called him, she enquired over dinner: 'Well, are you coming or not?' Perhaps he liked her forthright approach –

everything just seemed to fall into place from then on!

Not one to base her decisions on the attractiveness of the manse, Reta stayed in Edinburgh during the call, instead of measuring up for curtains! Her first view of Rosskeen was after Kenny had accepted the call, when they drove up for the Induction. Kenny and son Derek had been playing a football match on the way up, and they stopped in the lay-by before the church so that Kenny could change his clothes. Reta laughs recalling how Derek had urged her to drive off leaving the new minister stranded and half-dressed on the A9!

Reta also tells of the 'real coming to Rosskeen', when, at the manse, just before the induction, the late Davie MacLeod, who was then Session Clerk came up to the manse with the Session books.

'Davie prayed one of his beautiful prayers, and this tremendous excitement and anticipation gripped us, and this never left us – this expectation of God doing great things.'

Kenny was inducted to the charge of Rosskeen on 31st August 1984. He paid tribute to Rev John MacKay by saying that he inherited a congregation with a good base and in good order.

Kenny is quick to give all the glory to God for the things he saw happen in the following years. 'What I would like to get across is the wonderful way God worked in the area at that time. It was a time of great need and poverty. The Smelter had closed and Nigg was run down and many, many people were facing redundancy, unemployment and all the problems that brings. Many people came to church at that time – searching. God used these difficult circumstances to draw people to himself.'

**Roddy's Story**
'I was converted at the end of September 1984. It happened "out of the blue". I woke up one morning without a thought of God. My path crossed with an old school friend in the afternoon. He had been converted at a Billy Graham Rally the previous year. I don't remember a thing he said to me about being a Christian.

What I do remember was the impression that Christ was real to him. That brought me up short. I had boxed Christianity along with knitting woolly socks and butterfly collecting as something for old age or keen eccentrics. Now Christ was someone I had to face. I prayed to God that night before I slept and urgently asked for his mercy on my life. I received there and then a peace that my prayer had been answered.

Kenny MacDonald had nothing to do with this. He had been inducted, I think, the previous month. News of that event hadn't reached my circle, or if it had it was quickly dismissed as irrelevant. God has ways of making things relevant which we dismiss ourselves.

It was when I came home at Christmas 1984 from my first term of third year at Glasgow University that I first went to Rosskeen Free Church. I had a vague family connection with the Free Church although I don't remember ever attending any services. I had a friend with me who was thinking seriously about Christianity at the time.

I remember two things. The singing! James Campbell's haunting rendering of Psalm 119 v 89-96 to Palestrina has always remained with me so that whenever I hear that tune now I am back there in Rosskeen as an impressionable visitor. And the sermon! Kenny's passionate and solemn message about Ananias and Sapphira lying to God. This had a deep effect on me. A man who could weep as he pled with us to come to Christ was clearly someone who could teach me a tremendous amount about Christianity as a religion of the heart, a matter of divine love and utmost importance. To this day I retain the same impression of Kenny's passion for Christ. It has often been an inspiration when the fires of my soul were burning low. Even on the phone Kenny has the ability to send fire as well as his voice to you as though you were face to face with him!

After this visit I was hooked on Rosskeen as the place to go whenever I was at home. I was attending St. George's Tron Church of Scotland while in Glasgow, and the brilliant teaching ministry there was perfectly complimented by the evangelistic heart of Kenny's ministry.

I often found my times at home from university very difficult. It was a great help to be able to drop in to visit Kenny and Reta for fellowship. Their personal interest and concern made me feel like I was the most important person on God's earth. I'm afraid I didn't realise how busy they were and how many others there were looking to them for help, but I was never made to feel like I was intruding.

In the summer of 1985 I became convinced that I should serve God as a preacher and pastor, instead of following my chosen career in electronics. Again Kenny's role model had a part to play in that decision. The following February when I said I'd decided to enter the Free Church Ministry (if they'd have me!) Kenny got to work on getting me in right away. He always had more faith in me than I had in myself and quickly entrusted a Wednesday night prayer meeting to my leading. I still have the tape, but have never listened to it. I anticipate that the cringe factor would be too much for me! Hugh MacIver who, along with the rest of the Session also gave me great encouragement, found something positive to say: 'Don't be hard on yourself, I can see potential.' At that moment electronics seemed like the best option. If I'd expected everyone to be slain in the Spirit when I preached, it felt instead that my hopes of ever being a preacher were the only things slain. Perhaps, though, Hugh was right. I'd certainly never choose to do anything else now.

At that time I discovered that I hadn't been baptised as a child. So Kenny baptised me, received me into membership (by transfer from the Tron Church) and got me through the Session interview as a first stage to going to the Free Church College. It was the start of a roller coaster ride which I am still on. After graduation from Glasgow came my Greek language entrance exams from the College. I sat them in Kenny's study where there were plenty of Greek dictionaries beckoning when I got stuck. He trusted me not to use them and brought cups of tea to replace

the sweat the exams produced. 'How's "El Greco" getting on?'
he would ask. I suppose the answer is that I made it into College
thanks to Kenny's encouragement, not the dictionaries.

One feature of the early days of Kenny's time in Rosskeen
was that there were fellowships held in various homes where
the elders would help young Christians like myself to get on our
feet. I used to love going down to Donald and Janice Stirling's
with men like Lindsay MacCallum and Hugh MacIver for
fellowship. These were long standing Christians, yet they were
ready to let me have my say when I opened my loud mouth.
They also had a way of putting me right and restraining my more
outlandish notions. I think that they in turn derived
encouragement from what God was doing in bringing young
converts like myself into the fellowship. These mature Christians
were the foundation of the growing church and had been well
grounded in their faith under the teaching of the previous minister,
Rev John L. MacKay. I was always very impressed at how they
took Christianity seriously in every part of their lives and were
not afraid of doing difficult work for Jesus Christ.

It is very occasionally that I get back to Rosskeen these days,
indeed even while at College I was frequently elsewhere
preaching during the holiday time. So I have lost touch with
many of the friends there and with what is happening there these
days. I look back on my contact with the congregation and the
ministry there as being a lifeline to me in my early Christian
life. I certainly received far more than I gave, but isn't that the
way any fellowship should be towards its new Christians? I
wasn't judged, or pressed into a mould, but allowed to learn and
grow in a healthy way.' (Rev Roddy Rankin, Minister at Kyle of
Lochalsh)

## Ladies Prayer Meetings

'In November '84, a few months after Kenny and Reta were in
place, I received a phone call from Anne Wilkie to invite me to
a prayer meeting. This was to be a "test run" to see if there was

a place for a Ladies Prayer Meeting in Rosskeen. Apparently, Reta and Anne had discussed it, and Lillian MacKay and I were invited to go.

'I remember being in awe, because there had never been an all-female Prayer Meeting in Rosskeen. So much was happening – Kenny was full of ideas and vision. There was "life" and "busyness" but it was also scary, because here was something very new.

'I went for that initial meeting and found it was really good. We began with a reading, and then we had a time of open prayer, then some discussion about the way forward for this meeting. It was decided to go public and intimate it.... And so began the Ladies Prayer Meeting.

'We met every fortnight, and over the years it has changed very little. Sometimes you felt so overwhelmed by tears "when prayer was wont to be made" that it scared you a bit, and maybe you said in your mind that you wouldn't go back, but in your heart this work was sown, and so you were drawn back.

'The purpose of this small group was to pray for the work and people of the congregation, but over the years this often went world-wide.

'For all of us involved in the Prayer Meeting during Kenny's ministry, I would like to say the most humbling thing was the privileged information we were given concerning Alison. Alison held a very special place in the Ladies Prayer Meeting. If there was any new information regarding her whereabouts, we were told about it and we prayed accordingly. If a visit to India was planned, we prayed about that – and looked expectantly for an answer. In all these times when Alison did not come home with them, there was never once a hint of doubt. Reta was steadfast in her faith and belief. When you prayed alongside Reta you were very aware of her deep faith in Jesus, her love for him, and the fact that her much quoted phrase – "The Lord's mercies....they are new every morning" (Lamentations 3:22, 23) – was really how Reta lived. She looked to Jesus every day for his goodness.

Reta was so spiritual in prayer – we really miss her so much. We really were a very privileged group of women.' (Janice Stirling)

'I have fond memories of the Rosskeen Ladies Prayer Meeting. As a "young" Christian, I recall being constrained to pray, not only in privacy, but also with other believers. I approached the Ladies Prayer Meeting in the manse with fear and trembling, and yet with great expectation to pray out loud with women, not knowing them, but yet remembering that Scripture says we are "all one in Christ."

'The warm and loving welcome was not just sometimes, but always. Reta had a way of making you feel important for the task.

'There were times when you just knew that the Lord was there, and we would finish reluctantly because we would rather have stayed there. Time seemed to stand still on such occasions.

'Then would come a "blessing" and a welcome cup of tea. Sometimes Kenny would come in with really nice jam doughnuts, and would joke and say "the labourers were worthy of their hire!"

'All those things added to the joy of being together in prayer. And the example that Reta showed us, as wives and mothers, was of lasting benefit to us.' (Cathy Dunlop)

## Invergordon Sunday School

'We came to Rosskeen in 1979 and left in 1987, and over that time the outstanding memory is of how the Lord blessed the congregation with growth. Many different activities started over that time and we were both involved in the Invergordon Sunday School.

'When we came to Invergordon to live we had no car and we were dependant on others for transport. We were not the only ones in this situation, and the minister at that time, John MacKay, was aware of the need for services in Invergordon itself. Various venues were looked at and finally South Lodge Community Wing was chosen. Services started initially once a month and then increased to twice monthly and eventually became weekly.

'Once these services were established, it was suggested (I think probably at Kenny's instigation) that a children's work be started before the evening service. As the evening service was at 7.30, to fit in with this, the Sunday School was arranged for 6pm to 7pm.

'Information about the Sunday School was put round the houses and the schools, and on the first evening we waited and wondered, and gave thanks to God, who brought eight children along. Lillian MacKay helped David and myself. The numbers fluctuated, but gradually increased. Tom Cowie also taught for a while. We eventually normally had a class of younger ones (primary 4 and under) and then separate classes for the older ones – for boys only and for girls only. The boys were particularly lively, but at least they were hearing something of the gospel and we pray that the seed sown may yet bear fruit.

'Invergordon Sunday School can certainly provide one or two amusing reminiscences! Because of the liveliness of the kids, discipline was a constant battle!! As David was a teacher in Invergordon Academy, he was viewed (in a small way!) as an authority figure. However, towards the end of our time of involvement he was quite often away preaching on Sundays, so the kids used to come in and ask: "Is Wilkie here?" and if the answer was "No" they would go out for more reinforcements of liveliness!!

'On John Graham's first night of teaching the boys – before he knew important things like where the light switches were – one of his class switched off the lights and left John (alone!) in the gym in the darkness, with seventeen boys who included two sets of identical twins!! It says a lot for John that he came back for more!!

'One of the boys didn't want the learning process to be all one way and after Sunday School, as the congregation began to come in for the service, was found demonstrating break dancing to one of the elders!

'On another occasion some of the boys remained behind for the service, but afterwards one was heard to remark that he preferred the first Sunday School to the second!

'We were both involved in other Sunday Schools too – myself in the church and David in Milton, and we both remember and cherish the fellowship and prayer involved among all these leaders.

'We have enjoyed looking back on these times, and thank the Lord for the examples of how he can work. We pray that the Lord would be given all the glory, for although he used so many people, the power came from him alone.'

(David & Anne Wilkie, who now work in Ayr, where David is the Free Church Minister.)

### Elizabeth's Story

One girl who began coming to Invergordon Sunday School in the Wilkie's time was Elizabeth MacKenzie.

She recalls: 'What was being taught began to become real and not mere stories. No longer impersonal and distant, Jesus became as real to me when I was ten years old, as he was 2000 years ago when he walked on the shores of Galilee.

'I remember well the night I went on my knees and asked Jesus to come into my life as God and Saviour. It was following a Sunday School at South Lodge. I found myself no longer able to listen to God's Word and keep doing nothing about my relationship with him. I knew, even at that young age, that I was to commit myself to Jesus. After all I had learned, I knew I was a sinner and needed forgiveness. Only Jesus could do this for me.

'Having not been brought up to attend church regularly, Sunday nights were now spent having fun, playing games, singing and joking with friends. Not in a park, as you may think, but at Sunday School in South Lodge Primary School.

'Many of my close friends went, although for some it was mainly to enjoy the juice and biscuits offered at the end of the evening. I too enjoyed all of that, but amongst all the activity, my ears became alert to what was being taught by our faithful and patient Sunday School teacher. To this day, I am still amazed they all came back to teach such an unruly mob each Sunday. I can now understand grace in action!

'South Lodge provided the vital link in bringing me to know Jesus personally. I soon began to attend what I thought was the "big church"! Rosskeen has been a strength to me which I miss dearly now that I'm in Aberdeen, but I know that wherever I go and whatever I do, my God will take care of me – forever.'

Andy Weager and Jimmy Gunn took over as leaders when the Wilkies left. Malcolm MacLeod, Barbara Ham and Davy MacLellan also helped for varying periods of time. Lillian MacKay continued to teach until the Sunday School was discontinued. In 1995/6, services in South Lodge were stopped due to the lack of interest from the community. The only folk who attended were those who were already regulars at Rosskeen Church, and so, what was intended as a community outreach service, was not fulfilling its purpose. The Sunday School was linked with the service, and so also stopped. A concern for the children of Invergordon did not stop, however, and plans were already underway to introduce 'Campaigners'.

## Mission '85
In the first full year of Kenny's ministry, an evangelistic mission was held. The leader of the team was Rev Farquhar Renwick (now of Knockbain Free Church). His cousin, Catriona Renwick, from Lochbroom, by Ullapool, had just left school, and she joined the mission, prior to moving down to Glasgow, where she worked on a project for the homeless for five years. Also on the mission team was Derek Lamont, who had just finished as a student at Aberdeen University....! They began going out together some months later.

## Afternoon Fellowship

'After some informal discussion, some of the ladies were invited to attend a meeting in the manse to discuss how we could visit our older folk in their homes, and perhaps provide a monthly meeting for them.

'This was in 1985, and soon the first of these meetings was held in the Alness Hall. As well as OAPs, we also had some of our unemployed folk.

'Eventually we moved to the new hall at the church, where the facilities were better, and we could use the tables for their cup of tea, and make it as pleasant as we could.

'The Fellowship is one of the loveliest meetings to be involved in. The privilege of "serving" our older members of the congregation has been of great benefit to us all. Pouring a cup of tea is a great opportunity to ask someone how they are and make them feel welcome. The great thing about the Fellowship is that some of our "regulars" are outwith our own congregation, and have been with us from the beginning. They are a great encouragement to the folks who run the meeting.

'One of the best loved parts has been our little children who have been associated with the meeting. They have come along with their mums, and while that "important person" has poured the tea or passed the food around, these little ones sat and played and added greatly to the afternoon. The Fellowship has enjoyed watching Linda, Elaine, Rory and David MacIver grow up, and Hugh, David and Mairi Ferrier do likewise. We remember Scott Lamont in his baby chair, and Joe and Amy perched on either knee of Dad Derek, as he skilfully delivered his talk!

'And so this has been much more than a place to have a cup of tea and a blether – it's a place where the Family of Rosskeen met around God's Word, and shared that Word together. We heard speaker after speaker talk about their testimony or favourite psalm – or just plain gospel preaching, and all in the space of an hour and a half.

'We really have much to be thankful for.

'When I reflect on past days, one name keeps coming into my thoughts, and that is Miss Ella MacDonald. Ella was a lovely gentle person who was overtaken by a very debilitating illness, but did this keep her back? No Way! She would come to the Fellowship and cope as best she could, and enjoy being part of the company. Her gritty determination to be in God's House when she really was quite unwell shows how much she loved being with God's people and in the place of worship.

'Ella suffered from Parkinson's Disease and I always remember seeing her really in bad shape and yet she would quote: "I have learned to be content in whatever circumstances I am in" (Philippians 4:11). Whenever I read that verse in the Bible, I think of Ella.' (Janice Stirling)

The Afternoon Fellowship continues today, and is held monthly in the Church Hall, on Friday afternoons from 2.00 - 3.30pm. Transport is provided for all who require it, and all ages are most welcome.

'It passes a nice afternoon among friends and you get the spiritual message as well.' (Mary Manson)

'I enjoy the Fellowship very much. Everybody is nice and kind to me. We get a lovely tea – a lovely spread, and I get enough food home with me for my own tea.' (Bessie Anderson)

**Eldership**

In December 1985, Hugh MacIver, Simon Allison and James Campbell were inducted to the eldership. Roy MacGregor and Tom Cowie were appointed deacons earlier that year.

**The New Church Hall**

'I suppose, if the church at Achnagarron was to have been built today, or within the past fifteen years, it would have been built the other-way round. So, instead of the main door facing south-east, it would have faced north-west. The front elevation which is so much more impressive in its design and of quality workmanship would face the main carriageway north, the A9.

'Of course, the architects and the builders of the day could not have foreseen that the time would come when a new road would be constructed passing the rear of the church. The church was built facing the old A9, previously the B817, known as the back road to Kildary. The former A9 would take you round by Invergordon.

'The church built at Achnagarron crossroads is a prominent landmark, and it must have been a real privilege for all the tradesmen who were engaged in the work. They would have been extremely proud of their endeavours. The fruit of their labours has been looked on by many people throughout the last century with admiration and a sense of respect for a quality of workmanship which now belongs to the past and is no longer evident, generally speaking, in the construction work of today.

'We are a privileged people to have such a fine building to worship in. The building would probably have been simpler and much more modest, were it not for the bequests which were made. I believe, however, that it is important that a place of worship ought to be an attractive, and pleasant place to be in. The acoustics should be good. A place where we can come away from the world and its affairs, and draw near to God. Such a place is the Achnagarron Church.

'The main church area is spacious, seating approximately twelve hundred people comfortably, and yet, in contrast, there are only two rooms to the rear, known as the upper and lower vestries. The vestries were sufficient at a time when the Sunday School met at a different time to the church services, and at a time when classes were held in the Alness Hall.

'For the convenience of parents and children, it was at some stage decided to hold the Sunday school at the same time as the morning church service. This worked very well for a number of years, and the upper and lower vestries were used for this purpose. The congregation was much smaller than it is today, and therefore there were fewer children attending the Sunday School.

'In the late seventies, the number of children attending increased, thereby increasing the number of classes and teachers. This encouraging trend did cause a problem as far as accommodation was concerned and, as a result, one class was using the landing area at the top of the east stairway. Not a very satisfactory situation, but, there was no other alternative for some time to come, until it was suggested by Rev John L MacKay that the dirty black hole under the upper vestry, which was once upon a time the boiler room, be converted into a classroom. And so it was that two joiners and an electrician from within the congregation spent some evenings and Saturdays, and made a respectable classroom out of the dingy basement.

'In 1984 Rev Kenny MacDonald was ordained and inducted to the Rosskeen Free Church. His style, profile and ministry were tremendously effective in drawing people to church, and within a comparatively short period of time the membership was growing dramatically. Inevitably, the congregation and the Deacons Court were faced again with this problem of accommodation, a growing number of children, a growing number of activities, and inadequate room. By late 1985 something had to be done.

'The Deacons Court prayerfully considered the situation, and despite the fact that there was not a healthy bank account to meet the need, planned a new building, a hall with folding partitions providing three areas for Sunday school classes. The building was to be linked with the main church providing a much needed kitchen and toilets. Plans were drawn. The plans were submitted to the planning authority and were subsequently approved.

'In late spring of 1986 work commenced. From the very outset voluntary labour was willingly forthcoming. The foundations were dug out by hand, and volunteers, together with a joiner-contractor from within the congregation, progressed with the building of the new hall. In God's providence, the hall was built at a time when there were a number of young men temporarily unemployed as a result of redundancy, and they were happy that they were able to make such a valuable contribution towards the provision of a new hall annexed to the Achnagarron Church.

'The working day commenced no later than 8am. There was no stipulation that the unemployed men were required on site by that time, but they were there, willing and eager to busy themselves in the work that had to be done. Moulds were shuttered and all the precast concrete items such as sills, window surrounds, arches, lintels and copings were made on site. One of the unemployed men had worked in a precast yard and I will always remember how his first colour sample of concrete was perfect first time. The work proceeded. Other helpers contributed much, and there were some who came along after their day's work, and I am sure some of them could say that they developed new skills.

'But what I will remember most of all from the building of the new hall is not the actual construction work, but the spirit in which the hall was built. Where could one find a construction site where the Lord's blessing was asked when we would all sit down to a tea break? Where in our land would you find a group of workers stopping for ten or fifteen minutes and the talk would not be worldly? The conversation was of spiritual topics, of the sermons preached, of the Christian faith, and of how the Lord was working in the hearts of men and women.

'It was a time when each individual went about his task and carried it out "as to the Lord". The unemployed were content in their circumstances, considering the fact that the only financial help they were receiving was their dole money. They did it joyfully, and there was no apparent discontent and no bickering.

'It was a time that will be long remembered by all who were involved. The volunteers made a valuable contribution towards the hall's construction, but I do believe that each received a great deal more from their experience, not in financial terms, but just that it was a good time, a time when we could all say "The Lord is my helper, I will not be afraid. What can man do to me?" I am sure that all of us who took part could say individually, and as a congregation that the Lord did help; just as the Lord helped Nehemiah in the rebuilding of the walls of Jerusalem, so the Lord enabled us.' (James Campbell)

'The only answer to the rising numbers in our Sunday School was to build a new hall. This was a big decision, as we had little money and few resources. In fact, it was a step of faith, and nothing less.

'There is no doubt that if we trust in the Lord, he works – and work he did by supplying all our needs. For instance, there was a problem with making the arches for the tops of the windows. The late Hugh MacKenzie came along to give a hand, and this was his trade, so the job was done! Or again, at the start of one day it was commented how nice it would be to have the windows finished just to make the hall watertight, and by dinner time, there they were! And when we were forced to build the end wall in stone (which was hard to get), we heard that Dalmore Distillery had decided to knock down the big house, and we not only received our stones, but slates as well!

'A personal, and on reflection, funny story I remember was the night we gathered to dig out the foundations. We were duly partnered off – one with shovel and the other with the barrow. I was partnered with Angus MacLeod from Invergordon, a tall and slender built man. So I thought it wasn't going to be a hard night for me. I volunteered to do first stint on the barrow and we sauntered over to do the work. It is safe to say that was the last time I sauntered that night. When Angus began to wield that shovel, it was as if a JCB started work, and before I knew it, the barrow was full (and I mean full!). This went on all evening, with little or no breaks, and much and all as I tried to persuade him to have a turn on the barrow, he would just say: "It's no bother, I'll just carry on shovelling." So, it was with great relief that some two hours later and my arms two inches longer, we stopped!' (Donald Stirling)

'When we were quite small, our Dad was paid off from work just at the time they started to build the hall.

'We used to go to "help" in the afternoons. We had great fun with all the folks who were building it.

'It was a beautiful day when the hall went up. Lots of men came to help. We were invited up to Kenny and Reta's to help with the tea, as the men were going up there for tea. From the manse you could see everything. It was really exciting seeing nothing one minute and all the sides up the next! We thought that was it finished and asked Mum when the first service would be! Little did we know it was just beginning!

'When the men were working on the roof we had great fun. They used to lift us up on it. Everything was brilliant – working from the heights or playing in the sand. (They often found our buckets and spades buried in the sand for cement!!)

'We had a great laugh the day they put the toilet pans into the hall. Taff Jenkins picked up the pan and blew into it, he told us it wasn't a pan at all but a special trumpet. He had to do it again and again. Poor Taff was shattered trying to keep us happy!!

'We know that building the church hall was a very special time for lots of folk in the church and we have happy memories of that time ourselves.' (Linda and Elaine MacIver)

'These are my thoughts and memories of the building of the church hall. The year is 1986, the month is May, and I had been out of work on and off for one and a half years or so. You may not believe this, but idleness does not sit well with me, and on discovering that the hall was planned (in fact the plans had been passed and warrants granted, so there was nothing to stop the job going ahead except the shortage of a labour force) I volunteered to start as soon as I got the go-ahead.

'The man in charge was James Campbell and he duly pegged out the foundations, which I dug out. Now I needed help, but this was not long in coming, for a few people arrived to mix, barrow and shovel concrete for the foundations. Once the under-building was brought up to floor level, the under-floor – which is of concrete – had to be laid and this was achieved on one Saturday when a whole crowd of help arrived. What a day! It was like a huge family gathering. There was a lot of banter and good-natured fun, but that floor was laid in double-quick time, as well as being done properly.

'Then we started building the wooden frames and sheeting them, erecting them and then getting the roof trusses up. This job fell mainly to Murdo MacIver, Taff Jenkins, the late Hugh Mackenzie, Jock (from Dornoch), James Campbell and myself. Once we had the inner walls up, Donald MacIver started building the outer walls, one of which is built of stone which we cut into suitable sizes ourselves (although we were amateurs). I must say that help came from some unexpected places, e.g. in the form of building advice from Arthur Scott, the loan of a stone cutting saw from Billy Millar and other bits and pieces which proved invaluable to us.

'I feel I should also mention again the late Hugh MacKenzie, whose practical attitude, mixed with a great sense of humour helped us immensely.

'As with all workmen, we had tea-breaks too, but they were not just tea-breaks! We sat at our tea and discussed things – the discussions were almost always about the things that mattered most, e.g. points from a sermon someone had heard; questions that arose in our own minds; maybe a thought that occurred from a daily reading – it could be anything – and as one question was thrashed out to our satisfaction, another point would be raised. Some of these points were of course too deep for us and help was called in on these occasions. Very often we had to wait for an answer until our resident theologians called to see how work was progressing, these being the late Davie MacLeod, Rev Hugh MacCallum and Rev Kenny MacDonald. All three were a great source of encouragement to us all – not only to finish the hall, but spiritually as well, and I know the Lord blessed these talks to me if not to anyone else.

'As November was drawing to a close the hall was almost finished (even with all our talking) and I believe that at this point God said "Thank You", for on the very day that we were sealing the roof with the lead flashing, both Murdo and I were interviewed for jobs. I got the job (as did Murdo) for three weeks work – but I took it anyway and now more than thirteen years later I am still employed in the same place!

'How can any man say that God owes him something? I know I cannot, for I believe very firmly that God rewarded me in a material way, through my job, but the riches he has given me spiritually are indeed untold.

'I apologise to anyone I have not mentioned by name, but I do remember all those who worked on that job and I am glad that I met and worked with them and I hope that they don't feel that they have been taken for granted. I often give thanks to God for allowing me to work on that hall for I feel that I have received much more from God than Rosskeen got – and they got a Hall!' (John MacIver)

### 'Now Then Do It!'

Many people have reason to be eternally thankful to God for the way the Holy Spirit worked in their hearts through the winsome preaching of Kenny MacDonald.

On 21st January 1990, he preached from 2 Samuel 3:17-18. He explained that the text speaks of a time in Old Testament history, when the Israelites (the people chosen by God) rejected God's choice of king. Most of the people favoured Ishbosheth, the grandson of the disobedient King Saul. A small faction remained loyal to David, who was anointed by God to be king, and so there was civil war between the two groups.

'The Lord sent Abner to command them to give up all the fighting and turmoil, and make the right choice, so that peace would reign. As Abner delivered the message from God to turn and make David king, he urged them: "Now then, do it."'

Kenny preached: 'Our text is taken from Abner's argument

as he argued with the people and told them to change their allegiance from the king of our own choosing. We are called upon to give up the king of our own choosing. We are called upon to give up the ruler of our lives until now (that is, ourselves) and we are called upon to accept the King who is the one chosen by God – the Lord Jesus Christ.

'And although the text speaks to us all, I think it especially speaks to those who are swithering in their minds – those who have turmoil in their minds: they want Jesus as King in their lives, they want to be a Christian in some ways, but something holds them back.

'The Word of God is quite clear to you today, my friend. Whoever you are, wherever you are right now, the Word of God says to you: "Now then, do it!"

'This is a day for action! (Praise the Lord that we have lived to see it). For this command comes direct from heaven itself – not bound by man's systems, not bound by secret ballots, no time for negotiation.

'The Word of God goes out to you today with authority and power, and says to you: "Now then, do it!" The time for inaction, the time for swithering, the time for delaying, the time for hiding, the time for arguing is all gone – God says to you this morning: "Now then, do it!" '

### Assistantship

In a large and growing congregation, there can be a huge workload for one minister, and if necessary the Free Church can appoint an assistant.

In 1990 Rev Derek Lamont was appointed Assistant Minister at Rosskeen. Newly qualified from the Free Church College, he was well known to the congregation, having spent the previous summer preaching at Rosskeen while Kenny was away in India. He had also, of course, been part of the Mission Team in 1985, where he first met Catriona who had now become his wife. They had married in September 1989, and moved into the newly acquired Saltburn Manse in September 1990, where they literally kept an 'open house'. Catriona remembers that they were 'delighted' to come to Rosskeen.

## Care Worker

'My appointment as Congregational Care Worker in the latter half of 1990 was the brainchild of Rev Kenny MacDonald. Having spent over thirty years as a social worker in Manchester, I was looking forward to a quiet life in the Highlands, catching up at long last with my hobbies and staying well away from other people's problems. So when Kenny asked me, my heart sank to my boots and it seemed at the time that I was getting involved because I hadn't the courage to refuse! It is only now that I see it was all planned by the Lord.

'There were a number of formalities to be organised and there were discussions as to hours worked, payment etc. but finally, with the approval of the Deacons Court, it was agreed that I would keep to the professional conduct of a social worker with regard to confidentiality with the proviso that the minister only would be notified of my work. From this, it was agreed that all referrals to the Congregation Care Worker would be via the minister. Referrals would be taken from anybody in the community, not just the congregation of the church. Hours were to be flexible, visits either to the client's home or my own; the church would pay my out-of-pocket expenses with a review of the whole situation after a period of six months when a better assessment of what the duties would involve, could be made.

'No sooner was I in post than the Gulf War started. Because I was a stranger to the area, the impact on the community was lost on me, but gradually I began to realise the effect it was having within this small area, and that none of the official bodies were doing anything to help. The resources of Rosskeen Church came into full play at this time and everybody associated with the church at that time is aware of the benefits which it was able to provide. The church hall was opened once per fortnight for soldiers' friends and relatives to have a meeting place. The ladies of the Congregation provided an abundance of home baking with tea and coffee. There were flowers on the tables, the hall was warm and welcoming, and relatives were encouraged to share their worries and fears. A free parcel service was organised, members of the congregation sent parcels and wrote letters to any soldiers who had no relatives, and some of these soldiers actually took the time to reply.

'Thankfully, the war did not last long but the effect of the work of the church during that period is still remembered by the community. To this day, I am stopped from time to time by soldiers' relatives to enquire about the members of the church. Although some people resist entering a church, they will privately express their thanks for the help and comfort they were given.

'I have spent some time describing the previous events in detail because I believe that my appointment at that particular time was the work of the Lord and that he was showing all of us what can be achieved when we all combine the skills he has given us and use them to do good to others, all to his glory.

'Following the Gulf War, my work settled down into a fairly relaxed routine of visiting people at the request of the minister. Sometimes I have been able to assist in a practical way by liasing with officials to obtain grants etc. Sadly, there are sometimes problems for which there is no answer, and although I cannot offer a solution, I can offer friendship and understanding. It is a fact that people living under a great burden of sadness feel relief if they can talk about their problems. And with someone like myself, an outsider who is bound by the rules of confidentiality, they are able to express illogical feelings of anger, injustice, guilt etc. without adding to the burden already being shared within their circle of family/friends etc. The other asset I had was *time* and I was able to stay for as long as it took for somebody to get some relief, whereas people usually perceive the elders and minister to be busy and have a desire not to bother them unduly.

'These are what I would call the Social Work side of my

work for the church. During the quiet periods, I filled the gaps by visiting the elderly people who live alone, hospital visiting and just generally taking part in the fellowship which was ongoing in the church.

'The question of payment did crop up again but I found it impossible to cost my work. Most of my visiting I fitted in with my own running about to the shops, and the warmth and friendship which I received from people made it a pleasure to visit them. So any expenses which I occurred I put down as my extra tithe to the church.' (Opal Taylor)

At the time of writing the congregation does not have a Care Worker, but the work is being extended with the formation of a Pastoral Team.

### Newsletter

Rosskeen's first newsletter was printed in November 1991, and included this personal message:

'It is seven years since I became your minister. Reta and I have enjoyed our stay here very much. We, as a church, have known happy and exciting times as we have seen, and continue to see, the Lord's hand at work in our midst.

'We have also known sad times when the church lost some of her family – some called home to be with Jesus, others sadly gone back into the world. As I look forward to the future, my overriding desire for the Rosskeen Church is that there would be many more prayer meetings throughout the congregation and that they would all be well attended. Then the Lord would bless – then our church would be full to overflowing.

'May God bless you all.'

Kenny MacDonald

Later in the newsletter, an item welcomed sixteen people who had taken the step of faith and became members of the church during the previous June, August and November Communion seasons. The Lord's hand was indeed at work in our midst.

## Blythswood Collection Point

In April 1992, the church began a monthly collection point at the hall, on the last Saturday of the month.

Blythswood is a Christian International Relief Aid Organisation collecting and transporting essential supplies directly to adults and children in need in countries including Albania, Bulgaria, Romania and Russia. The items requested were lentils, flour, pasta, rice, corned beef, powdered milk, salt, soup, sugar, coffee, tin openers, baby food, nappies, blankets, sheets. Money was also collected (it costs over £3000 to send a 38 ton truck to Romania).

Mr Jock MacKinnon organised the collections from the church and delivered the goods to Dingwall after each collection.

We are very grateful to Jock for his faithful commitment.

## Mission '92

'The Kirk Session has agreed to the request of the ministers to have another Highways and Byways Mission in Rosskeen in the summer of 1992. The original team members are being written to and asked to help again, and it is hoped that some of them, as well as other young people in Scotland, will come and help. Farquhar Renwick is to be the leader of the team once more.

'The last mission was a great success and it is hoped to reach many new people with this renewed effort. The mission will be from 15th to 31st August 1992.

'Please make this work a matter of diligent and urgent prayer, both publicly and privately. May it be a focus for a revival of religion in this area, and an encouragement for ourselves as a congregation to work with the team as a team.'

Kenny MacDonald
November '91 Newsletter

'Prior to the mission there was a great deal of excitement and anticipation in the congregation. At prayer meetings the issue of the mission always came up and people prayed fervently that the Lord would bless this work and that the power of the Holy Spirit would be felt. The Great Romance of the last mission prior to this in 1985 was often mentioned and people wondered if any other young people on the mission would meet their life partner! (For anyone who is wondering who I mean, it was of course Derek and Catriona.)

'Both of the manses were full to bursting with young people in every corner. It was obvious that the young volunteers all had close relationships with their Father in heaven and were very keen to try and share the peace and happiness that they had found with other people.

'At the time of the mission a number of teenagers had links with the congregation. The youth fellowship regularly had over thirty teenagers attending. 'The Place' in Alness became a meeting point for teenagers during the mission. This was continually full and many who came had never been involved with the church before. I remember a few things from times of fellowship at 'The Place'.

'One is the time an ex-prisoner gave his testimony. I remember being amazed that here was a man who had committed a terrible crime being completely at ease because he knew that he had found forgiveness for his sins through Jesus Christ. It really brought it home to me that everyone of us is offered forgiveness and peace and that it is no excuse to say that you are not good enough to receive it.

'A second, but perhaps a minor thing was that snacks became free on a Sunday. I think this was an excellent witness to the young people.

'As the mission was held over the summer it was also the season for services at 'The Burn' – Ferintosh. These services were really special and a lot of the young people from the church went along. I think that this coupled with the mission produced a real closeness and unity amongst all of us and is something upon which I still look back with very happy memories.

'The culmination of the mission was a Communion weekend. I had thought about becoming a member at Rosskeen at the previous communion but I did not wish to rush into it. However, that August I knew that it was time to make a public profession of faith and become a member of my second family.

'The presence of the Holy Spirit was often evident during the mission and the work certainly bore fruit. It was wonderful to witness the closeness of the people at Rosskeen and the way so many people worked together because of the love of their Lord.' (Claire Armstrong)

'Alongside congregation members, the team included Farquhar Renwick (leader), Louise and Neil MacMillan, Mary MacMillan, Fiona Boyd, Rhoda Renwick and Chris Smart.

'Over a busy week, the activities included Games Nights at "The Place", Alness, with testimonies from church members and the mission team; a barbeque at Ardross for children; Door-to-door visits, and Supper Evenings in the church hall, with one particularly geared for inviting work colleagues. Rev Neil MacLean gave an epilogue at one of these suppers.

'One lasting activity in Rosskeen's weekly schedule began its life during this mission. There was a marquee up at the manse which was being used for sleeping accommodation and for youth meetings. It was decided to use it for a special Mothers and Toddlers Outreach Event. Friends were invited for food, play, fellowship, singing and a brief epilogue. It was a success, and a second Mothers and Toddlers event was held in the church hall.

'Soon after the mission, Catriona Gunn, Marion MacLeod and I met to discuss and pray about setting up a weekly Mother and Toddler group in the congregation, the aim being to give Christian mothers the opportunity to have fellowship with each other and also to invite their non-Christian friends to come along, with their children. The group took the form of chat and play, then juice and eats, and finished with some gospel songs and an epilogue, particularly geared towards those without Christ. The three of us took it in turns to give the talk, although sometimes a Bible story was read to the children.

'Thus, the Mother and Toddler group at Rosskeen was established and is still going strong.' (Dorothy Hannan)

One busy mum who has reason to be thankful for the Mums & Toddlers Group is Mhairi Stirling.

## Mhairi's Story

'I was born and brought up in Invergordon. When I was very young I went to Sunday School, but don't remember learning anything (I think I went for the sweets!). I went through school not really grasping what I was being told about the Bible, although I've always believed there was a God.

'I was married at seventeen, and within eight years had my four children. My marriage ended after ten years.

'During those years, I attended church a few times, again not hearing anything about what the Lord had done for me. Today I know worldly things were blocking my ears. I know now to pray about those things. A lot has happened to make me realise that there really is a God, and he cares about me.

'At Mums and Toddlers I listened to the talks, and loved being among Christians who liked me the way I am.

'After the break-up of my marriage, I really went off the rails. But after a few months something drastic happened, and the Lord showed me what it would be like if I carried on that path. He took me and put me on the right path, through Psalm 40, which means so much to me today.

'After a few weeks of feeling settled I decided to go to church. I phoned my sister, Catriona Gunn, but there was no answer. An hour later, she phoned and asked me if I'd like to go along with her. I could hardly believe it – the Lord was working in my life once again. I went every Sunday after that, and took in every word.

'Then I got the chance to go to the family camp, which really opened my eyes. If all these lovely people were Christians, then I really wanted to be one. Some friends at camp bought us a Bible, and written on the inside cover was John 3:16. I looked this up, and read it, and cried.

'When I came home, I was so spiritual – all I wanted to do was talk about the Lord. The following Saturday I prayed: I asked to be saved, and to be forgiven for all my terrible sins, and I took the Lord into my heart.

'When I awoke the next morning, I felt disappointed that there was no ray of light shining on me. Later in church, Kenny preached about what I had expected to see. He explained how people get their signs from the Lord in different ways – not always dramatic. I believe Kenny was my sign, saying I was accepted. I will remember that day forever.

'Today, things are not always easy, but I have the Lord to help me. I love my children – Michelle, Nicole, David and Scott – dearly, and we are very happy having the Lord in our home. He has blessed us with great happiness and lovely friends.

'God bless you all.' (Mhairi Stirling)


**Janice's Story**
'I am so thankful for those who prayed at this Mission time. We knew nothing about it, but I am sure that God answered their prayers by working in our hearts to bring us into the Rosskeen branch of his family. What happened to us at that time was so profound and so deep, that it is very difficult to describe. Words cannot begin to express the way God touched the deepest parts of our beings.

'In early 1992, aged twenty-six, I had a miscarriage. Although the pregnancy had been unexpected, once it was established it was much wanted. To lose the baby left my boyfriend and me shattered.

'We were not church goers, in fact I was very much into New Age ideas, and regarded Christian beliefs as outdated and irrelevant. However, despite myself, I found myself worrying that my miscarriage had been a judgement from God, because we were not married. It was quite amazing, because although my head dismissed this as crazy thinking, my heart could not. It played on my mind and I decided to go to church, thinking I would please God by just turning up. We went to Rosskeen in May 1992, because we had heard vaguely that the minister there was a good preacher – and we had seen many cars parked outside. We were quite overwhelmed by the friendly welcome we received – we hadn't expected the congregation to notice or value us, but we were instantly invited to dinner with three different families. Even the minister sought us out for a friendly blether! The only other thing I remember was his extraordinary purple patterned kipper tie!

'Despite the warm welcome, our interest in church was put on the backburner for a few months, but I did a lot of thinking. Could God really be up there? What does happen when we die? I felt sure that our baby must have had a soul – otherwise, how could I explain how devastated I felt, if all I had lost was a piece of tissue? That horrible word "fetus"! It wasn't a "fetus" to me – it was a wee person – our baby. Was? If the baby had a soul, was it alive somewhere now? But where? With God? I had no answers, and was very disturbed by these issues. However I knew with certainty that my soul had been touched. As my own 'philosophy' believed that I didn't have a soul, the rug was suddenly pulled out from under all I had previously believed.

'When we next went to Rosskeen it was August 31st, (unknown to us, just after the Mission, when the congregation had been praying for people to come in). It was a Communion Service. I wasn't listening to the sermon, but I suddenly heard Kenny say: "Would the Lord's people come and take their places at his table." For a short time no-one moved, and I thought to myself, "Ha! See! No-one's interested in this religious stuff anymore." No sooner had I thought this than I was proved wrong, as in the next moment all the people around us stood up as one and moved together to take their places at the tables.

'I was stunned by this and thought: "Something is really happening here." It was as if I was suddenly "woken up" spiritually for the first time in my life. I was powerfully aware of the presence of God in the building – I didn't see him or hear him, except that there was a beautiful brightness, a sort of glow all around where the Communion tables were. It was unlike anything I had experienced before. I knew it was God. I suddenly knew clearly that he was making himself known, just to me, and I was terrified. It was like Judgement Day and these people were his people, but Davy and I were on the wrong side. I grabbed my Bible for help, not knowing where to look, but I turned to a psalm we had already sung – Psalm 40. I read verses 11-13:

"For ills past reck'ning compass me,
and mine iniquities
Such hold upon me taken have,
I cannot lift mine eyes:
They more than hairs are on mine head
Thence is mine heart dismay'd.
Be pleased, Lord, to rescue me
Lord, hasten to mine aid."

'The language was difficult, but as I read I knew exactly what the words meant. They could have been written just for me; they exactly described how I felt and my situation, and they were exactly the words I needed to say to God right then. I knew that God was helping me to recognise for the first time that I was a sinner. I thought of my pride, my selfishness – my sins were indeed more than the hairs on my head. "Lord, rescue me," I prayed. Because he had given me the words, I knew that he would accept my prayer. My fear lifted, and I knew everything was going to be alright. He did "hasten to my aid." I didn't realise exactly how everything could be made alright – I found that out later. At this point I just believed and I felt at peace with God –

something I realised I had never felt before in my life.

'I was weeping, and turned to a very shocked Davy, and announced: "You'll have to marry me!" After almost falling off the pew, Davy put his arm around me gently. I could tell by the look in his eyes that he knew something major had happened. He can tell his own story, but within the next week he also knew that God was speaking to him, and that we ought to get our lives in order.

'The next Sunday Kenny preached a sermon about not judging others. On the way out we asked Kenny if we could speak to him, intending to ask him if he would marry us. He was very friendly and took us up to the manse. As he led us into his study we felt very nervous and wondered what reception we would get when this minister found out we were living together. To be honest, we were half expecting to be thrown out! We needn't have worried: before we could open our mouths, he leaned across his desk with a big grin and said, "So you want to get married." We were most relieved, and Davy said afterwards that the love Kenny showed us had a huge effect upon his decision to become a Christian. Kenny's attitude was totally consistent with the sermon he had preached. We were married three weeks later!

'One evening, while up at the manse arranging our wedding, Kenny asked us: "And how is your relationship with God?" Stumbling over my words, I replied "We don't really have one, but we want one." "Keep your eyes on Jesus", was his simple answer. As we drove home, I pondered what he had said: "What did that mean – keep your eyes on Jesus? What had Jesus done for me?" As I asked the question, an image of a man on a cross burned into my mind. Just like that – quite simply, no emotion, just my answer, "Jesus died on the cross for my sins."

'That was how everything could be made right with my Heavenly Father – Jesus had paid the price for my sins, instead of me. I was free!

'Well, we couldn't get enough of church after that! We went to every meeting that was on, even attending a Presbytery meeting one night with all the ministers! I don't know if we were allowed to be there or not, but nobody said anything, although there was a room full of raised eyebrows when we walked in! We were never away from the manses and we pestered Kenny and Derek with all the questions which kept coming up ("What about dinosaurs, fossils, the age of the earth, other faiths, suffering?" etc, etc). Patiently, they answered all our questions, sometimes pointing out that we don't have all the answers, that some things are a matter of faith. Kenny often taught us: "Faith is a muscle – the more you use it, the stronger it gets." He advised us to make the most of our first year of being Christians as the Lord would be especially close, and that closeness should be stored up in our spiritual memory banks, because at some point God would withdraw a little and leave us to walk on our own for a time. These would be learning experiences, and we would learn to walk by faith.

'Kenny and Reta were so kind to us as we shared our thoughts with them. They listened with such care and interest that we felt very at home and very valued at Rosskeen. We learned a lot about Christian love from them. In fact, at Rosskeen we received a sound and loving discipling as baby Christians, from the congregation as a whole. We shared happy fellowship at the Saltburn Manse with Derek and Catriona and other young Christians. A particularly fond memory is the Christian Basics Bible Study, where a living-room full of people met to learn the basics of the truth of God. On dark winter nights, with log fires, mugs of tea, and chocolate biscuits we listened, we talked, we debated and pennies dropped. There was great freedom to ask and to question; there was much joy and laughter, and we shared such close times of prayer that we just did not want to leave.

'We were also invited into the homes of many families in the congregation – for Sunday dinners, week day suppers, and for cups of tea. We felt so welcome and so at home, and all the time we were learning more about our loving Saviour. All we wanted to do was find out more about God and what he has said – in the

Bible, from other Christians, from sermons, from Christian books. Many people who knew us were amazed and some were sceptical, as we had been pretty wild-living people! But, for us, the change in our lifestyle and our desires was infinitely change for the better.

'We learned how Jesus had changed other lives as well. Everyone had their own story. God works with us as individuals, meeting each one at the point of their need.

'Now we have been Christians for seven years, and as we look back we can see that our whole lives have been a journey. Even though we didn't know God before, we can see that he was there all the time – protecting, caring and guiding our paths from childhood, through the wild years, to settle in the parish of Rosskeen, and to meet with him there. Between us, Davy and I have lived in dozens of different places, and yet God brought us together when we needed each other most, and then brought us to himself.

'Being a Christian doesn't guarantee the old "bed of roses." Since we became Christians, we have had a hectic life, being blessed with three children in under five years. I have been ill with post natal depression twice. Davy has coped with redundancy, going to college and beginning a new career. We have had some major life changes, some dark times, some uncertain times, and our new faith has been tested. But God has been there with us, and has worked all these things for our good.

'He is our rock and our solid foundation.

'Each new day is a precious gift and we learn to trust in him to provide for our daily needs, which he does richly and abundantly. To know that the God who spread out the heavens and placed the stars in their positions, numbers every hair on my head and knows my every thought before I think it, is an inexpressible comfort. He loves me with a love that is perfect. I know that because he laid down his life for me. I can speak to him anytime. He is never too busy, and the Bible says that he loves to hear my prayers! What an amazing thought! We don't know what the future holds, but we do know who holds the future.' (Janice MacLellan)

## New Christians

Becoming a member in the church is not at all a matter of filling in a form, paying a subscription, attending for a certain length of time, or being on a committee. Becoming a member is the result of the Holy Spirit of God working in your heart, so that you see the Lord Jesus Christ as he really is – your Saviour, because he died on the Cross for your sins. This means that the price of your sins is paid, and you are free of it, and free to worship God as your Father, and to live in his house forever, when your life on this earth is over. It means that you are saved from a lost eternity. A member is someone who has committed themselves and their life to Jesus Christ and his cause, and who have decided to stand up and be counted among his people.

The following figures show how people heard and answered the Lord's call on their lives in Rosskeen over the last two decades of last century. We praise him and thank him for his goodness and mercy towards us.

'We pray that God will continue to use us to increase his Kingdom, and that in the years to come, the church will indeed be filled to overflowing.

| DATE | MEMBERS |
| --- | --- |
| 1980 | 25 |
| 1986 | 72 |
| 1987 | 113 |
| 1990 | 130 |
| 1994 | 176 |
| 1998 | 179 |

The membership rose higher than this between '94 and '98, but these years saw a great deal of coming and going, as a good few much loved brothers and sisters moved away from the area. One such family is the Morisons. Here's what they have to say about Rosskeen.

'Rosskeen represented a refuge for us at a time when we were tired and a bit "stressed out". Until we moved to Rosskeen church life had been too hectic. Travelling was an increasing problem and we were stretched. At Rosskeen we found a place where we could slot in without being in too much demand, but with plenty of opportunity for service.

'However it only took eighteen months for Rosskeen (and Kenny MacDonald) to make the ultimate demand of us. "Go to the Free Church College" is a rather extreme way of getting rid of folks, but it worked!

'So we moved, in full confidence of the support of our sending church – a support that has now even extended to your sending us additional help in our new area of service in Elgin! (Donald and Janice Stirling moved to Elgin.)

'Looking back at our reasons for moving to Rosskeen, we feel especially grateful to people who come from a distance to support the services. Knowing the costs of commuting to church we appreciate the efforts made by others to do the same.

'We remain profoundly thankful to God for our time in Rosskeen, for the support received while there and since, and for the continued friendship and fellowship in the gospel which we hope to enjoy for many years to come.'

Colin, Christine, Cailean, Sam and Katie Morison. (Colin is now minister at Elgin Free Church)

## Elders

In May of 1993, three new elders were added to the Session, namely: Donald Stirling, Murdo MacIver and Andy Weager. Subsequently, it was felt that the time was right to renew and create distinct elders' visitation districts, in order to facilitate a regular system of visiting.

The congregation had grown a great deal (with 174 members

alone), and there was a real need for more widespread visitation. The congregation was encouraged to pray for the elders as they undertook this work (a great commitment), that it would lead to closer fellowship, and greater pastoral care and oversight from the spiritual leaders in the church. We were asked to make ourselves known to our elder, if we didn't know him well, and to make him a special subject of our prayers. We could approach him about congregational matters or personal difficulties, especially if we needed to be visited, or wished his help, advice or prayers, or those of the ministers.

## Men's Meetings

At the AGM of 1993, the popularity of the Ladies Meetings was noted by some of the men. The women had the benefit of many interesting speakers, good fellowship and the opportunity to bring along a friend, as well as excellent baking! A motion was put to the women of the congregation that the men be allowed to attend the Ladies Meeting also. The reply was a very tactful silence. Kenny asked, 'Well, does this mean the answer is No?' Again, silence was the loud reply and so the motion was rejected! The women felt that there is something very special and valuable about relaxing in and enjoying the company of other women.

So the men began their own Men's Meetings, run along the same lines as the Ladies, having a guest speaker and a time of informal fellowship. They could thus enjoy all the benefits previously enjoyed by the women (except that their baking is not quite so good!).

## Ardross Church

Back in 1899 the late Charles William Dyson Perrins, who contributed so much to the communities of Ardross and Alness, decided to build a church at Ardross as a thanksgiving to God for the recovery of his wife from a serious illness.

The building was opened on July 12th 1890, according to an inscription in the large Bible in the pulpit. The church was to be used by the people of the estate as a place of worship, under the Trusteeship of the ministers of Rosskeen Free Church, Rosskeen Church of Scotland, along with their respective session clerks, and the proprietor.

The conditions of the Deed are as follow:

Ardross Church Trust Deed

1. Mr Perrins conveys the ground and buildings to be vested in the trustees, viz, himself, Church of Scotland minister and Free Church ministers and their successors.

2. Conditions
   a. To keep Church etc. in good repair at all times.
   b. To maintain fence around church in good order.
   c. To be used only as church and graveyard. If sold, not to be used for any purpose disagreeable to Dublin people.
   d. Not to be sold or disposed of without first being offered to Mr Perrins or successor.
   e. If conditions not fulfilled, Trust is null and void and building reverts to Mr Perrins or successor.
   f. One shilling per annum as feu duty to be paid.

3. Use of Church
   a. Divine Worship according to forms of Church of Scotland and Free Church. Free Church have use of church 3 Sundays out of 4, Church of Scotland one out of 4. This can be altered to 2 Sundays each out of 4.
   b. if either fails to hold one service at least in 2 months, it shall forfeit their right to worship there and right to trusteeship. If both fail in this respect, the property reverts to Mr Perrins or successor.
   c. Trustees responsible for expenses involved in upkeep, cleaning, lighting.
   d. Trustees to insure building against fire.

e. Church only to be sold to buy or erect another church in locality.

f. Trustees to meet at least once per year.

g. If a minister declines to be Trustee, Mr Perrins or successor may appoint replacement.

Thus, the building does not belong to either church, but to the people of Ardross.

Until the estate was sold in 1937, heating and lighting was provided free. Lighting was supplied from a generator at Ardross Castle and heating by two large coal burning stoves. The trustees also received £5 per year for the maintenance of the building.

Mr Perrins resigned his office in 1941 although the £5 continued to be paid until after the Second World War.

Times changed, Ardross' population dwindled, as did the revenue, which was augmented by the Free Church and the Church of Scotland. The church fell into disrepair and due to their own financial burdens the churches were unable to add their aid.

By 1971 the trustees had no money available for the upkeep of Ardross Church. The building was dark, damp and cold. Slates and stones needed replacing and windows mended. In 1972 a Public Meeting was called at which the position was explained by Rev A Howe. The trustees saw that the only way to keep the church in use was for the community to make a wholehearted effort to raise money for the necessary repairs and subsequently to raise money annually for day to day expenses. By a show of hands it was decided by the people of Ardross that the challenge be accepted. A committee was formed and subsequently a Board of Management appointed. In Easter of 1973 a service of thanksgiving was held. Ardross Church was once again habitable and warm.

Since then, the building has been made weatherproof; re-pointed where necessary; broken rones and drainpipes replaced; broken windows (mainly stained glass) repaired; the old heating stoves removed and electricity installed to provide heat and light.

Day to day expenses of the church and cutting the surrounding grass are both carried out on a voluntary basis.

Services take place every Sunday – the 1st, 4th and 5th Sundays of the month by the Free Church and the 2nd and 3rd Sundays by the Church of Scotland.

Recently, Mr J E Thom, the treasurer of the Ardross Church Board of Management, met a descendant of the late Mr Perrins, who was delighted, on his first visit to Ardross, to find a church built by his ancestors, looking so well cared for. A few days after his visit, this Mr Perrins sent a most welcome gift to boost Ardross Church funds.

Keeping the building in a reasonable state of repair is an on-going process. Recent work has included some necessary cleaning and re-pointing of part of the stonework.

Despite very poor attendances, the Board of Management are determined to keep the services going.

(All of the above material is used with kind permission of the Ardross Church Board of Management.)

Poor attendances or not, the Holy Spirit is at work in Ardross Church, as testified by Trisha Black:

### Trisha's Story

'It was a Sunday afternoon in June '94 and I'd just arrived back from a Saturday night partying in Alness. I had been partying every weekend since Hogmanay. However I was not satisfied with my lifestyle: to work all week and party all weekend and so on, month after month, did not feel enough. Don't get me wrong, it was fun, but it didn't bring me lasting joy or contentment. So I'd just drink more and more and forget the discontentment until Monday, and then just try to forget it again in time for Friday.

'However, one Sunday, the Lord had more in store for me than the usual shower, hangover and cruise round and round Alness High Street!

'I was just in the door and Mum caught me: "You're coming to church." I mean, surely she'd got the message after three years of "NO!" I'd occasionally go, just to keep her happy – usually it just bored me, but sometimes it made me uncomfortable.

'However, this time, apparently, my twin sister Pam's new boyfriend was going to do the preaching in Ardross Church. Also Pam's mate Paula was going and she wasn't into the church scene either. It seemed polite to just go along, and anyway, the guy didn't seem too bad for a Christian, so I agreed.

'The first thing that struck me was the stained glass window of Christ on the Cross with a face of sorrow. I remember thinking about my life and world, and how he had died on a cross and nobody cared.

'Then Murdo (Pam's boyfriend) preached on Psalm 119 verse 105: 'Your word is a lamp to my feet and a light for my path.' He spoke of how the Bible is a guide to life, and how the Lord is the one who gives direction. So often people are like climbers on a hill in thick fog, he said – the Lord and his Word (the Bible) are the light and the path.

'Well! Never had a sermon seemed so right and so clear. A light had gone on in my heart. "These people have got it!", I thought. "They know the purpose and the meaning of life!" I had just been stumbling my way through life. But enough was enough. Now I knew what to do to have lasting joy and contentment. And I was delighted.

'After the service I felt a huge drawing towards these Christians. I wanted what they had, and asked if I could go to the Evening Service and the Youth Fellowship afterwards. I mean, for someone who cringed and shied away from Christians before, I suddenly felt so at home with these people.

'It caused a bit of concern among the girls when I had to decline the offer of cruising because I was going to church. They hoped I wasn't turning all funny on them. However, they had to admit that they'd never seen me so happy, and asked would I still hang out with them. Of course I would – I loved them, and now I had a deeper love for them in my heart, which was from the Lord.

'The Lord never promised an easy path in life. I've since known very happy times, but also known much sadness too. But he has promised to direct my path and guide me and keep me through my life. I've known his presence, love and protection every step of the way, and I know that I'm walking home to the open arms of Christ – not always walking, but more often than not falling and stumbling, but he always lifts me up and leads me on.' (Trisha Black)

## Minibus

'It was the hottest teabreak topic – the company (United Distillers) was getting rid of all the minibuses and their employees were going to have to use their own cars for transport to work. This was the second time I had been in a group and the conversation revolved around minibuses – the other group being the Deacons Court at church where the discussion had been on how the church really needed one. Now the news at work seemed to be the answer to our transport problems and prayers, but I was still a bit apprehensive about mentioning it at the Deacons Court. After all, the kirk and the whisky industry weren't the closest of friends! Anyhow, I did, and after a very thorough discussion it was decided to pursue the matter prayerfully. If it was not to be, then the Lord would stop it.' (Donald Stirling)

On Wednesday 22nd June 1994, a local paper reported the hand-over:

'The delighted minister, the Rev Kenny MacDonald said he had no reservations about accepting the minibus from a whisky producing firm. He said: "Strong drink in its place is there for man's use and man's enjoyment. It's not bad in itself – it's the abuse of strong drink that's bad. We are a scattered congregation and we have a lot of activity at the church all week involving young and old, so it'll be a great help to have our own transport.'

Wildon Campbell and Kenny MacIver gave the diesel minibus

a thorough overhaul – mechanically and bodily. The re-spray job was done and after a good clean it was up and running, thanks to Donald Stirling, being God's man in the right place! The minibus is still well used today and we are very grateful to United Distillers.

## Davie MacLeod

In the spring of 1995, to our great sadness, we lost our beloved Davie MacLeod, who passed on to be with his Saviour. A local of Alness, and well known and respected, he was such a part of the congregation and served faithfully as an elder for thirty-six years.

He loved his Saviour, God's beautiful creation and all the people who had the pleasure of knowing him. He passed on only good things about others because he was a man of peace.

The Newsletter noted: 'In sadness, we rejoice, because we know that Davie has been welcomed into his everlasting home, and is singing God's praises there now, just as he ever did during his life here.'

Our mourning was made easier, knowing that Davie was now fulfilling his own greatest desire – 'to gaze into the eyes of Christ.'

'My wife and I became Christians in September '92, and in the following months, five of our good friends also committed their lives to Christ.

'One of the people at Rosskeen who made the greatest impression on us was Davie MacLeod – "Old Davie", we called him. He was one of those people you meet, whom you immediately love like your own grandfather. He welcomed us into the church that he loved with his gentleness and warmth and sincerity and wisdom and love.

'He and his brother Walter visited our homes often, and invited us to his, along with his wife, Helen. He would relate wonderful stories of his youth spent as a farm worker. His love for the horses he worked with was plain, and his memory for detail together with his descriptive talents meant he had our full attention.

'But it was as a spiritual adviser that we treasured him most. His wisdom, always delivered with care and gentleness, and his humble example, set out clearly the path ahead for us as young Christians.

'He was always dressed well – comfortably, but neatly. We, on the other hand, were a bunch of scallywags – rough and ready, piled into the back of an old pick-up van to go to the church, and tumbling out dressed in our jeans or any old way. Yet we never got the feeling he thought our dress or behaviour inappropriate, even although he was brought up in a more respectful era when more importance was attached to one's mode of dress for church. Quite the reverse in fact: "It's so wonderful to see the young people in the Lord's house", he would say. We felt not just accepted, but very much wanted and valued.

'As young Christians we learned from and were edified by his prayers at the Prayer Meetings. "Did you hear Davie's prayer last night?", would be heard in many a gathering. Not only was the content of his prayers memorable, but by his reverence and the awe with which he spoke, we knew he was speaking to a Holy God.

'He was a great and gifted precentor of the psalms – even today, it is often said in discussions of the singing: "I do so miss Davie's precenting."

'Davie was such a wonderful observer of the creation. He would find such beauty in his surroundings, and would watch and wonder with a keen eye. He knew the nesting site of each bird in the thick hedges of his garden, and observed the details of their comings and goings with the amazement and pleasure of one who knew their, and his own, Creator. He had a gift of seeing the miraculous in the ordinary things of life, often praised God in his prayers for the everyday miracles others take for granted. Truly, he was a man who gave all the glory to God.'

(Davy MacLellan)

'The passing of faithful Christians from our congregational family reminds us of our own mortality and the urgent need for our souls to be ready to meet with our Maker and Judge when he calls. As sinners we need a great Saviour, and as people we need to experience the only love that can wrap around us for eternity. Otherwise we remain eternally lost and searching for the sublime satisfaction of the forgiving and filling love of the Lord Jesus Christ.

'The cry from the lives of those we love who are now silent in the Lord, and of the desperate pleading from the pulpit in Rosskeen is:

"SEEK THE LORD WHILE HE MAY BE FOUND,
CALL ON HIM WHILE HE IS NEAR."

Derek Lamont, Newsletter May/June '95

**New Elders**
That spring, Kenny MacIver and David Lipp were added to the eldership.

**New Resources**
The beginning of 1995 saw the Church Library begun, with people donating books to fill its shelves. Those who use it often are very grateful for the availability of commentaries, study guides, biographies and other material.

Another resource was made available to us that year, with the idea of the Video project. No sooner had the matter been raised in the Deacons Court, than a video camera was supplied. It seemed that the project had the Lord's blessing and Donald Stirling was the very man to iron out the finer points of the organisation. The project was up and running by the end of July, with all sermons being taped, and a delivery service offered for the housebound. A video library was soon built up, and is situated at the front door, alongside the cassette taped sermons.

**Alness Mums and Toddlers**

Throughout the summer of 1995, Marion MacLeod had increasingly felt that the Lord was guiding her to start up a second Mums and Toddlers Group in Alness. The idea was prayed over by several people, and Marion asked the Deacons Court for the use of the old Alness Hall. It was in quite a grim condition, and reservations were expressed, not the least being safety, as the electric wiring was in poor condition. Some repairs were done and the walls were given a lick of paint. Marion and her friend Shirley Chalmers from Alness Baptist Church opened the doors and waited to see who the Lord would bring along.

She is very anxious to give the Lord the glory for what happened: 'It was obviously the Lord's work. The surroundings were certainly not congenial, but the need was there, and the Lord brought people along, and they really supported each other.' The facilities remained poor and with the involvement of Margaret Morrison (whose husband Ronald is the minister of the West Church of Scotland in Alness), the group moved to the West Church's Hall, where it continues today. The move was more suitable all round, being in easy walking distance for most of the mothers who were coming along. The group is now run by Anne Ferrier, together with Margaret, Anne Marie Wallis and Kathryn MacLeod.

**Kenny**

Kenny MacDonald is a remarkable man in so many ways. It is impossible to meet him without being impressed by the love of Christ shining in and through him. He speaks the truth of God with boldness, and will never miss an opportunity to cut through conversational niceties to enquire about the state of your soul. But he is such a warm and loving person that he could never cause offence by such enquiries, even to the most private or most hostile person. One of his gifts is his incredibly crazy sense of humour. Those of us who thought Christianity was a dry, staid affair soon had our misconceptions blown away.

Kenny's antics held him in good stead in his pastoral duties. The Gunn family were most impressed by the new Free Church minister when, on leaving after his first visit, the three boys, Lewis, Steve and Gary, observed him out of the window doing the Highland Fling in their garden!

Kenny also treasured what he called 'the priceless gift of bad taste' in clothes, and was quite infamous in the local schools for odd socks, purple shoes and garish ties.

The most important thing about Kenny is his love for the Lord Jesus. What he desired above all for others was that they would also come to 'know the man from Galilee', that they would see the loveliness of the Saviour. We remember his tears as he pleaded from the pulpit: 'Do you know the Lord?'

It was said of Kenny that the Holy Spirit especially used him to speak to those who were secret believers, those who were Christians but did not publicly profess it because of perhaps a lack of understanding of what the public profession of faith at the Lord's table is all about. In the Highlands there can be a cultural attitude which says: 'I am not worthy; I am not good enough to take communion at the Lord's Table.' Kenny's teaching enabled many who had long watched the proceedings from the sidelines to understand that *no-one* is worthy, except for the Lord Jesus Christ. That is the whole point – the Lord's Table, the church, the Christian faith, are for sinners. The only requirement for taking part in the sacrament is that you *love the Lord*. We love him because we have come to understand that he gave himself up on the cross, for us, even though we are unworthy, because *He Loved us*.

### Alison

Kenny and Reta are able to accept the situation regarding Alison's disappearance, because of their trust in a loving God. The Bible tells us that all things work together for good for those who love the Lord. The Christian trusts in God, even when the circumstances are hard to understand. 'The one who has the mind of Christ does not necessarily understand all mysteries. Maturity is the ability to carry the unanswered question in faith. It is more important to obey than to understand. It is more important to believe, than to know' (Elizabeth Elliot).

The MacDonald's belief that their trauma is part of God's plan gives strength but does not take away the pain. 'We know, we honestly know, it's going to be good in the end, although we are temporarily and desperately hurt.' Nineteen years is a long time, humanly speaking, but God does not work to our time scale. They point to God's active intervention, even in the search, like the wonder of being able to travel to India eighteen times, although starting off as a penniless student. 'Whenever it becomes necessary to go, somehow the money comes in, even when people don't even know what we are contemplating. And always there's just enough to do what's needed. Somehow the Lord just provides.'

Neither is it a question of closing their eyes to the worst-case scenarios. 'We have looked realistically at all the reasons she could be missing, but have been preserved from them. We have been given the strength to look them in the face and move on, without the scourge of constant speculation,' says Reta.

'I've even searched for her body in the river', confirms Kenny, 'so it's not at all a question of closing our eyes. It's more that we've examined things in a rational way, and then moved on without being overloaded with pessimism. We've been spared too much speculation though, and that's important, because to speculate constantly would drive you mad.'

Their loss has been a means of blessing for others. Liz Merry, who was Alison's travelling companion in India, has since become a Christian, as have many other people who have been moved by Alison's story. Kenny describes how his own experiences have given his sermons a particular kind of credibility with members of his congregation facing other crises. The book which was written about her seems to have been able to be a source of real comfort to many people, even parents having to cope with the suicide of a child.[1]

Over the previous months it had been obvious that Kenny's health was deteriorating, but it was still a dreadful shock when he announced his intention to retire in the spring of 1995, after being diagnosed as having multiple sclerosis. Although he felt well physically, he lost the sight of one eye completely, and the sight of the other was reduced to a very small circle of light.

It was hard to accept that this was God's chosen course for Kenny and Reta, and for us as a congregation. As always, Kenny and Reta themselves provided us with a model of how to exercise our faith at this time. Speaking at the annual Afternoon Fellowship outing (that year it was to Strathpeffer) the newly-retired Kenny MacDonald reminded us that as Christians, we may go through difficulties we may not understand, but in Isaiah 40:31 we are told 'they that wait upon the Lord shall renew their strength.' God is in control. If we look to the Lord he will guide us.

Kenny told journalist Ruth Wishart in the same article: 'Well, it's a completely new existence of course, with a special gluten-free diet. But you can't spend your life worrying about things you can't do anything about. Our life has never been a gradual sliding into the next phase – it's always been a complete change. And if we receive word that Alison is at a certain place, then I'll get there. If it has to be at a slower pace, I'll get there. The fact that I've got MS wasn't my own fault, so I'll just wait and see what the Lord plans to do.'

## Kenny's Retirement Evening
When Kenny was forced to retire, he and Reta did not want the focus to be on themselves, but on Jesus.

It was a very special family gathering with the church packed with friends from all over the country. Although we met to

---

1. This material is taken from an article in "The Scotsman Weekend" by Ruth Wishart, 14 May 1994, and used by kind permission.

express thanksgiving and praise for all God had done through Kenny's ministry, it was Kenny's desire that it would not be his evening, or our evening, but the Lord's evening.

It took the form of a Praise Evening, and we sang from the Lord's songbook. Kenny and Reta chose psalms, each portion having a special memory or significance for them.

Mr Duncan Gordon, an elder with the Free Church Fortrose Congregation, led the singing.

The first psalm reminded Kenny of a Communion Service in 1985 – he had been at Rosskeen for one year. 'It was very moving for a new minister to see the people rising from every corner of the Church to sit at the Lord's Table, especially so this time, as there were fifteen new members that day (and a total of thirty-seven in that year – many of whom are pillars of Rosskeen today). As they came down from all the corners of the church they were singing Psalm 118 verse 15 – the words Jesus himself would have sung at the Passover – words of triumph and joy and confidence, obeying the Lord's command, 'Do this in remembrance of me.'

'In dwellings of the righteous
is heard the melody
Of joy and health: the Lord's right hand
Doth ever valiantly.'

Then Kenny recalled a special time of preaching from the book of The Song of Solomon, associating it with Psalm 45, which speaks of the church as the bride of Christ. He notes that in verse 10 there is the separation of Christ's Church from the world. This is commanded, and we are told that then; 'Thy beauty to the king will then delightful be.' And in that psalm we have a picture of the bride being adorned in glorious array. J C Ryle – Bishop of Liverpool last century – said, 'He was stripped of his clothes, so that we could be clothed in righteousness. He was given thorns, so that we could be given a crown of glory.'

Many of the psalms are notable for encapsulating our complete Christian experience, like Psalm 130, where the psalmist has a consciousness of sin, and then a consciousness of God's mercy and God's forgiveness, and a consciousness of hope and redemption.

The familiar verses of Psalm 143 v 6-8 can surely be echoed by the believer who has learned to wrestle in prayer and has learned to trust in God's faithfulness in hearing prayer: The words here are words that Kenny always uses in evangelistic services, chosen because of their encouragement to people to reach out to the Lord:

> 'Lo, I do stretch my hands
> To thee, my help alone.'

In Psalm 124 we have a glorious expression of the believer's awareness of God's grace and sovereignty – the sovereignty of Almighty God over his people's lives and affairs. We see here God's everlasting arms in all situations – IN ALL SITUATIONS – a gentle, comforting Saviour.

We note, particularly, the psalmist is looking back over his life with assurance and confidence, and he is able to say, 'Yes, this is how God dealt with me', and so may it be with us as we daily realise that God had dealt kindly with us even when we are not aware of it.

> 'The raging streams with their proud swelling waves
> Had then our soul overwhelmed in the deep
> But blessed be God who doth us safely keep…
> Even as a bird out of the fowler's snare
> Escapes away, so is our soul set free
> Broke are their nets and thus escaped we.'

Kenny says he has always looked on Psalm 23 as "The Sunshine Psalm". There is the picture of a shepherd, with his sheep, in sunshine. And truly we have in this psalm a picture of heart peace, of soul peace: the pastures are green, the waters are quiet, the soul is restored, there's a rod and a staff to protect, there's a cup overflowing with the goodness of God and there's an eternal dwelling with him for the believer.

During the course of the evening, Rosskeen Treasurer Roy Harmon, well expressed the sentiments of us all as he made a presentation from the congregation to Kenny and Reta: 'It is more or less eleven years to the day since you came here and were inducted on 31st August 1984. Those years have passed very quickly, and there have been many changes in the congregation in that time – we are grateful for them all. An occasion like this must be tinged with a degree of sadness and regret in that you are going, and that the reason for your retiral has been brought about by your failing health with respect to your eyesight. That is a matter which is of great regret, but it is not in our hands – these things are in the Lord's hands, and we must accept his will in all things. But we have the comfort that God does all things well, and that all things work to the good for them that love him.'

Then Kenny spoke. After thanking everyone for coming, he continued: 'It is very difficult to speak on a night like this, and Reta said to me as we were coming down, "Don't be frivolous," but I'm afraid, all my life I've never been able to separate the frivolous, that is, the ludicrous from real life, because that's how real life is – there's the ludicrous side and there's the serious side.

'It is interesting how we finished up here. I know it's the Lord's Providence that I was late in going in for the ministry, yet I can look back now and see that every step of the way was just a preparation to come and preach the gospel in Rosskeen. We were particularly suited to one another, and our time together has been blessed by the Lord. I always found you real people – that is, there was no veneer of respectability about you (and that doesn't mean that you are not respectable, but it was a real respectability!). The good thing about that was that it kept my feet absolutely upon the ground.

'I remember some emotional times, but I also remember some ludicrous times. I remember preaching once in a place not very far from here, and preaching well (as I thought!). I went around the old people afterwards to ask them if they'd heard the message, to check up on whether they had heard and understood what I had said. I came to this little old lady who was smiling sweetly, and had an absolutely scrubbed face – it was lovely and red – just like my mum she was. She wore a little fringe collar and just looked a lovely picture. I came to her and asked if she'd heard the message. "Oh, yes," she replied. 'And you understood it?', I asked. "Oh, yes," she says, "And I'll tell you what you are – you are a blethering twit!" I had to come down and preach in Rosskeen after that, but only after a very strong cup of coffee.

'There were emotional times too. I remember the hall being built out there. One day there was nothing but the foundation and the next day the hall was raised. It was amazing how people were unemployed until the work was finished – then they all got work immediately afterwards. That was a very moving time for me.

'One of the other things I remember was challenging the pupils of Obsdale School to learn Psalm 23. They took up the challenge and I went back within a month and they sang it for me, just like children do – absolutely joyfully and joyously, and it really shook me. I have always had special affinity with Psalm 23 as a happy sunshine psalm, and it was very emotional to see the little kids there, from the youngest to the oldest, singing it without any notes or any help at all. They just sang it from the heart. Things like that stick in your mind.

'There were sad times too, we won't dwell on them, but the congregation know them – times when the Lord was very near and took some of our friends away. But we bow before him, and we recognise that, over the years, he has blessed us in a very special way, because there were years when we didn't lose anybody. And that's very unusual for a Highland congregation. Also we've had more births and baptisms in the church than anything else. It's a tremendous blessing. It must be very demoralising for a minister to come to a place and find that he's losing more than he's bringing in.

'The position of the church is peculiar, being beside the main A9, and I honestly don't think there were many days when there weren't any visitors among us, particularly in the mornings. It is a good place for picking up passing trade!

'The only advice I can give the congregation is to love their minister, and to love one another as the Lord Jesus Christ says "Love one another as I have loved you, and by this shall all men know that you are my disciples, if ye have love one for another."

'I know you are in good hands: Derek has been trained for six years, and the only advice that I can give him is that he should buy a coloured hanky (referring to his habit of using large bright hankies in the pulpit),' At this, Derek duly produced a red hanky from his pocket and Kenny laughed: 'That's it – you are in capable hands!'

After the summer, Kenny and Reta moved to the old Free Church Manse in Resolis, where they work alongside Rev Donnie and Debbie MacDonald in Ferintosh and Resolis Free Church. When he was asked what role he saw himself playing in that church, his reply was: 'My job is to make them laugh.'

They named their new home 'Sonamarg', after the village from which Alison disappeared.

# CHAPTER 7

## REV DEREK LAMONT

After Kenny retired and he and Reta moved away, there was inevitably a short time of uncertainty in the congregation. Derek, as assistant minister, stood in Kenny's shoes, while the Presbytery and congregation met to determine the will of the people regarding who should be the new minister. It was a great night when the congregation gathered together under the Interim Moderatorship of Rev. Neil MacDonald, Fearn, and unanimously voted that Derek should be the new minister. There was a great feeling of the Holy Spirit being among us, and guiding us. Mr MacDonald's pleasure at the united will of the congregation was obvious. (As far as we were all concerned, there was, of course, no other choice!)

Derek was born on 9th January 1964 at home in Kilmallie where his father, Rev. Donald Lamont, was the Free Church minister. Six months later, Mr Lamont, his wife Joan and their young family were called to St. Columba's Church in Edinburgh where they were to settle for twenty-five years.

Thus Derek grew up in the Capital with his brother Peter, and sisters Barbara and Anne, leaving as a teenager to study Business Studies in Aberdeen. Derek then completed a post-graduate course in teacher training before his life took a turn in an unexpected direction. He then found himself called by God to apply to the Free Church College to become a minister. His Free Church pedigree is impeccable with both his father and his maternal grandfather, Rev Farquhar Matheson, having served as Moderators of the church.

**The Induction**

On Tuesday 14 November 1995, the induction of Rev. Derek Lamont as minister of Rosskeen Free Church took place. The church was packed full with our own congregation, friends from other congregations and the families of Derek and Catriona. It was a great pleasure to be part of this occasion. There was an air of reverence and praise to God, of joyful excitement and of great hope for the future of the gospel in Rosskeen.

The evening began with a short sermon from Rev. Donnie G MacDonald (Ferintosh). The Holy Spirit reminded us, through the sermon, that our future as a congregation in Rosskeen depends not on any one minister, or upon any one man or woman, but upon the word of God and our faithful witness to the world.

Then Rev. Neil MacDonald, the Interim Moderator, gave some Biblical advice to the new minister and to the congregation. He recalled the episode in the book of Joshua on the eve of the assault of Jericho, where Joshua meets with the Lord, who has a drawn sword in his hand. With Moses gone, Joshua was now no longer the apprentice. He had the whole responsibility on his shoulders of directing the campaign to conquer Canaan. This was a daunting task, but the Lord had already given encouraging promises to Joshua, such as:

1. 'As I was with Moses, so I will be with thee.'
2. 'I will not fail thee, nor forsake thee.'
3. 'Be strong and of a good courage' (Joshua 1:5-6).

The Lord was the Commander in Chief of the Great Campaign. This also is our encouragement in the Lord's work. He is in control and holds the sword symbolising the great guarantee of success.

Mr David Lipp (elder) welcomed Derek and the new lady of the manse on behalf of the congregation. As he presented them with a gift and flowers, he asked God's blessing on them, their family and their ministry amongst us. He then read out a card with the following text as a message:

"Only be thou strong and very courageous, that thou mayest observe to do according to all the law, which Moses my servant commanded thee: turn not from it to the right hand or to the left, that thou mayest prosper whithersoever thou goest. This book of the law shall not depart out of thy mouth; but thou shalt meditate therein day and night, that thou mayest observe to do according to all that is written therein: for then thou shalt make thy way prosperous, and then thou shalt have good success. Have I not commanded thee? Be strong and of a good courage, be not afraid, neither be thou dismayed: for the Lord thy God is with thee whithersoever thou goest" (Joshua 1:7-9)

with love from Kenny and Reta.

Then we were handed over to our new 'gaffer', and Derek thanked the congregation for the gifts. He explained that it was not easy to step into the former gaffer's shoes, as Kenny was a hard act to follow. Speaking fondly, he recalled how, early on in his days as Assistant Minister, he noticed that people bowed in reverence as Kenny approached. Derek was impressed at the respect Kenny commanded, until he realised that people had been staring at his purple shoes!

Derek spoke lovingly of his own father, being so glad of his presence that evening, especially as he had been unable to attend his previous induction due to ill health.

He went on to speak about his vision for Rosskeen's future. Together he hoped we would go forward on three important foundations:

1. Prayer
2. The word of God.
3. Evangelism.

Hugh MacIver (elder) then made a presentation to the Interim Moderator, Rev. Neil MacDonald. He thanked him for what he had done and for the gracious manner in which he conducts himself in all he does.

The worship was appropriately closed with Psalm 133, which reminds us of the unity we enjoy and pray will continue. The celebration and fellowship continued as we enjoyed the fantastic spread of food provided. The catering committee once again worked so hard to serve us all, splendidly ending a unique and happy occasion, a treasured memory for all present.

## A Note From Derek

'I would like to express my real and deep appreciation for all your support and prayer for me and the family during the unsettled time of change towards the end of last year. The sense of unity and willing helpfulness has been a great encouragement, and not a lot could have been achieved without it.

'There has been a great deal of change in Rosskeen in a short time, and sometimes I don't think I have fully taken in that Kenny and Reta are no longer formally part of the congregation. Thankfully they remain concerned for us and they, along with Alison, continue to be prayed for in the congregation.

'Over the next few months, we in the Kirk Session are going to prayerfully consider all the activities under the umbrella of the congregation. There has been a tremendous growth over the last ten years, and it seems only right that now, as the opportunity has afforded itself, we move forward in every area with conviction, vision, direction and a clear spiritual purpose.

'In a small congregation, everything is very easy to "manage", but as a congregation grows, just as in a family, more organisation is needed to put everyday spiritual responsibilities into practice. At the Prayer Meeting we are looking at Nehemiah – he PLANNED for action.

'A spiritual vision is so vital because if we aim for nothing we are sure to achieve it – NOTHING. Our great vision individually is to be as like Christ as is possible, by his grace. The same is true for us as a congregation.

'My prayerful vision for the church is very old fashioned – nothing new, nothing fancy; a simple pattern, based on the New

Testament church. It can be summed up in four words –
PRAYING, CARING, LEARNING and GROWING.

'These basic spiritual principles for the church have been the
core for generations in our country, since the Reformation. How
they are put into practice in Rosskeen is our task and
responsibility today.

'I have a great deal to learn. We are all dependent on the
leading and guiding of the Holy Spirit, and if we are to be blessed,
then we must each take on board our responsibilities, recognising
that we are people who have to give account of all we have done.

'There must be partnership and a willingness by us all to
serve. I hope and pray, with the elders, for the wisdom and love
to serve the congregation with my sleeves rolled up. I seek a
continuation of the support and unity that the ministry has enjoyed
in Rosskeen for many years.'

Derek and Catriona moved out of the Saltburn Manse and into
the Rosskeen Manse, but the "Open House Ministry" continues.
Both are truly and totally committed to Christ, and their lives
are dedicated to sharing their love for Jesus with others. The
manse door is always open, visitors are always welcomed and
hospitality is always generously provided. With three young
children themselves, the home is usually alive with children
tumbling around, making it a lively and a happy place to be.

Derek is very aware of his responsibility to the wider church,
and is much in demand for Communions, Missions, Conferences
and other preaching engagements. Then there is the full schedule
of events in a typical week at Rosskeen, around which he
organises his pastoral visits. He coaches youngsters in Obsdale
Primary (where Scott, Amy and Joe attend school) in football
skills and regularly takes assemblies in most of the local schools.
He has been very involved since its beginnings with the Thomas
Chalmers (now Calman) Trust in Invergordon, which provides
supported flats for teenagers in need.

Catriona, too, is involved in a busy programme of work

including two Campaigner groups, Mums and Toddlers, a Bible Study, the Young Women's Prayer Meeting, the Ladies Meeting and the Youth fellowship.

Summer holidays come around and Catriona and Derek run Free Church Youth Activity Camps for a break!

When they do have holidays, they often head 'up the west' to help Catriona's dad, Fachie Renwick, on the croft, enjoying outdoor physical work such as the lambing, as a contrast to the demanding work of pastoring the flock at Rosskeen.

The family are avid Ross County supporters and are to be found at Victoria Park whenever possible.

Derek's style of preaching is passionate, emotional and energetic. He is inspiring and urgent, always pushing his hearers to move forward, to strive to be ever closer to Christ, exhorting us to deeper devotion and committed service. We must be constantly examining ourselves in our Christian walk – not remaining still, becoming stagnant and complacent, but moving, onwards and upwards, maturing in the faith. Above all, he seeks to glorify Christ.

His fervent plea is always for people to recognise their need of Christ, and to come to his ever-open arms. He urges non-believers to "Taste and see that God is good" (Ps. 34:8). Derek committed his own life to Christ, when, as a teenager, he became convinced of the truth of the Bible.

Today, his testimony remains that the words of God are:

More to be desired than gold,
yea, than much fine gold:
sweeter also than honey
and the honeycomb (Psalm 19:10).

**Student Placement**
Students training in the Free Church College were by 1995 required to undertake a placement with an experienced minister at the end of their first year of study.

We were delighted that in the summer of 1996, one of the students was placed in Rosskeen. This was a particularly welcome development, as we were without an assistant.

Grant MacAskill, who hails from Fort Augustus, was with us officially from 20th May until 2nd July, but agreed to stay on until the end of August, to cover for Derek and Catriona being away running a Free Church summer camp and then taking a well earned holiday.

Over the period of Grant's stay, he was involved in all the variety of congregational life as well as preaching. He was popular with the Youth Fellowship, in demand for giving his testimony, and was even brave enough to lead the singing at Mothers and Toddlers.

Right from the beginning, Grant was much loved by the whole congregation for his gentle and sensitive preaching, which was used by the Holy Spirit to comfort and uphold many. Janice Maclellan particularly remember having gone through a difficult time, and Grant preached on Psalm 51, where the writer of the Psalm is penitent and restored by God. Psalm 51 was much used at that time and the words which Grant spoke finally enabled her to close that chapter of her life and rest in the joyfulness of being restored to a right relationship with God.

"Do thou with hyssop sprinkle me,
I shall be cleansed so;
Yea, wash thou me, and then I shall
be whiter than the snow.

Of gladness and of joyfulness
make me to hear the voice;
that so these very bones which thou
hast broken may rejoice.

All mine iniquities blot out,
thy face hide from my sin.

Create a clean heart, Lord, renew
a right spirit me within.

Cast me not from thy sight, nor take
thy Holy Spirit away.
Restore me thy salvation's joy;
with thy free spirit me stay (Psalm 51:7-12).

We were all glad to welcome him back for a six week spell in the summer of '97, to assist Derek and to cover his holidays. Grant often joins us for worship when he visits his parents in this part of the world. It is always a pleasure to see him and to remember the blessings we shared under his ministry.

Grant is now a Youth Worker with Dundee Free Church. He is a man of many gifts, and we pray that God will use him mightily wherever he leads him. May he be assured always of a warm place in the hearts of the people of Rosskeen.

## Hamish's Story

Hamish MacDonald tells us how he came to know Christ as his personal Saviour.

'Sorry, no blinding light or thunder and lightning, just the passing of time (a long time).

'I was born in Newmore, which was a small estate in the early 40s. I cannot say, with my hand on my heart, that my parents were Christians, but it was a happy home. They pointed me to Rosskeen Free Church Sunday School and attended church regularly.

'I enjoyed myself like most youngsters in the 50s and, though I had the feeling that God was ever near, I didn't think too hard about him.

'Being a "loner", I lived in this world but many things passed me by. Cycle racing became part of my life but God kept "bothering" me by popping into my mind at the queerest of times, even during the races.

'I now know that God put a crack in my heart and, like a crack in a piece of granite during the passing of time between rain and frost, the crack became bigger and his Spirit began to push everything else out.

'Things at work went well, and now and then I had an elated feeling of how well I was doing. But every time this feeling came the phone would ring and this was to let me know something had gone wrong. God in his grace never let me fall too far. Now I say a silent prayer to him who helps me at all times. During the last number of years God entered my mind more and more. I used to think that communion was for the good people but Derek kept on preaching about the tables being for sinners like me. To die without Christ began to horrify me. I made up my mind to go forward one Thursday night but chickened out. That night I awakened with panic in my heart. Satan seemed to be pulling me towards him but the decision to follow Jesus was made. I'm now a young Christian but nearing my 'sell by' date. My favourite Psalm is 137.'

## Outreach in Milton

The work in Milton began in 1980 under the auspices of Fearn Free Church. Ian Paterson from Balintore was one of the founders of the work, and remained very much involved, even after 1986 when, due to parish boundary changes, the work in Milton came under the control of Rosskeen.

In the beginning services were held as well as Sunday School and Games Nights. The services were unfortunately discontinued due to lack of interest.

The Games Nights ran on Friday nights during school terms, from 7.30pm to 9pm. These were usually well attended, with between thirty and fifty coming along. Ages ranged from four to sixteen. We gave a short gospel talk at the beginning, with various ordinary Christians coming along to share their love for Jesus with the children.

The Sunday School went through a difficult period, with

attendances only averaging seven or eight, although we were encouraged by occasional attendances of up to twenty-two children. We suffered a break in continuity between August '92 and May '93 due to the non-availability of premises, and attendances suffered consequently.

The Games Night leaders were Hugh MacIver, Murdo MacIver, Gary Matheson, Richard Stirling, Kevin Stirling, Hugh Kirkwood, Christine Morison and Davy MacLellan. The Sunday school teachers were Hugh MacIver, Wildon Campbell, Kenny MacIver and Richard Stirling.

In September 1996, the work in Milton and Invergordon changed direction. Attendances were poor at the Sunday Schools, and the Games Nights were difficult to organise and to control due to the large numbers and the wide age range of those attending. The solution? 'CAMPAIGNERS' !

The newsletter of that month noted: 'Tremendous thanks are due to all those, some who have put in many years of work, who have taught and helped at the Milton and Invergordon Sunday Schools. Their work has been, and continues to be, absolutely invaluable. It is our sincere hope and prayer that the Word sown in the hearts of these youngsters will bear fruit in years to come.'

## Campaigners

In September 1996, we were delighted when two Campaigner groups got underway – one in Invergordon and one in Milton. It was hoped that the work would extend to Alness the following year.

Campaigners is a national evangelical Christian youth movement. It is not a Free Church organisation and is recognised by most Christian churches. The purpose of Campaigners, in all aspects of its varied programme, is to bring the Good News of the gospel of Jesus Christ to young people. The Campaigners programme is based on the belief that 'unstructured youth work quickly loses its freshness, discipline and motivation. Young people benefit from the security, authority and challenge a structured programme provides, and youth leaders benefit from the continuing resources, ideas and freshness of an up to date relevant programme.' (Campaigner chiefs manual)

Three years on and Campaigners continued to thrive. By the beginning of 2000 there were three Campaigner groups: Invergordon Junos ( P2 -P5); Milton Junos (P2 – P5); Invergordon Inters (P6 – S1).

'We meet on Friday evenings in the respective primary schools. Currently the Invergordon Junos is regularly attended by thirty plus children, most of whom have limited church background. There is even a waiting list for those wanting to join.

'The night usually starts with registration and a wee kick about with a football. Then the fun begins. We open with drill, which everyone enjoys!!

'Then we have games, followed by tasks, when each group, with their own leader, do something different. These range from skipping, cooking, sewing, using tools, to learning about the Royal family, laying a table, keeping healthy or national costumes.

"Clan C" is the serious part of the night. All the children sit in a "C" formation and are told a story about Jesus. Every "Clan C" starts with a quiz to see if they were listening the week before. The night is rounded off with juice and biscuits.' (Richard Stirling, Junos Leader).

Each term an outing of some kind is planned. These have included a trip to Victoria Park to see Ross County playing, a pool party at Invergordon, a trip to the Aquadome in Inverness and a grand barbeque in the summer term. It is good fun when all the groups meet up together for these occasions.

Campaigners and their families are also made very welcome at church services. The whole congregation enjoys the prizegiving and family services, when the front six pews of the church are filled with the Campaigner children in their smart blue and red uniforms.

The Campaigner work is very close to the heart of the Rosskeen congregation, and is constantly upheld in prayer. From its beginnings in John MacKay's time, outreach to the children of the area is a vital part of our efforts to share the love of Jesus. We pray that the seeds sown will have blessings eternally.

## Youth Worker

The proposal for Rosskeen to have a Youth Worker first came up at the congregational AGM in February 1996. An evangelical organisation called Careforce enable 'volunteers and suitable congregations to be matched up for a year'.

At that time Derek was frustrated by how little quality time he felt able to devote to developing the work among the young, and to addressing their spiritual needs. The appointment of a Youth Worker, working with the minister, would be beneficial in meeting these needs.

All that was needed was the right person to become available, the necessary financial requirements to be met by the congregation and accommodation to be provided. That was all!

After the meeting, nine people committed themselves to additional weekly financial support. This was taken as a sign that the Lord wanted the project to go ahead. The next stage was 'Pray On'....

As it turned out, the demand for Careforce workers that year out-stripped the supply. In fact, fourteen congregations did not get the help they applied for and Careforce were very apologetic. We hoped and prayed that there would be enough suitable volunteers for the next year to meet the increasing need to take the gospel to our young people. The Kirk Session, however, were greatly encouraged by the willingness of the people in the congregation to support the venture financially.

In the summer of 1997, everything fell into place and Ricky MacDonald became Rosskeen's Youth Worker. Ricky had just finished a theology degree at Aberdeen University. He had been president of the A.U. Christian Union the previous year, had been actively involved in Bon Accord Free Church, and was well known to several of our students.

The Newsletter reminded us: 'May we all pray for guidance (for Ricky) and for God to bless our efforts to engage more full-time workers. We know there is a spiritual harvest and we have asked the Lord of the harvest to provide more workers. He has done this – we must take up the challenge with faithful commitment and EXPECTATION.'

For the first year Ricky stayed at the Rosskeen Manse. His work initially included leading the Youth Fellowship, taking a young people's Bible study and Prayer Meeting, being a Campaigner Leader, planning outreach and visiting the young folk. It was very encouraging when four schools approached him with a view to being involved in Religious/Moral Education classes. Plenty to do!

Ricky quickly became very popular not just among the young folk but among the oldies too. A quietly spoken, gentle and humble man, everything he does is soaked in prayer. Ricky's knowledge of the Bible is thorough and detailed, making him a wise counsellor and a sincere friend.

In June 1998 Ricky and his fiancée Melissa were married. Melissa was soon enlisted as Campaigner leader, Sunday School teacher and, together with Ricky, hosting the Youth Fellowship and such like.

In September '98, Ricky wrote a letter to the congregation keeping everyone informed of their work:

'It has now been over a year since I came to Rosskeen and it is no longer just another place, but my home. It is a great place to start off in married life. Melissa and I know that the Lord has really blessed us in giving us such a good start.

'First of all, I would like to thank you all for your prayers and support over the last year. It is good to know that our loving God hears and answers prayers.

'The year gone by has been a very eventful one for me – starting youth work, getting used to a totally new area of Scotland, meeting so many new people and of cousre getting married...

Please pray for me as I work, particularly in the schools as that involves a lot of preparation and is such a great opportunity to bring the Good News to so many kids who have never heard it before.

'Thank you for your prayers

Ricky.'

## Assistantship

At the end of 1996, the Kirk Session was in contact with the Free Church Foreign Missions Board regarding Mr. David MacPherson.

At that time, David was a final year student who hoped to return to full time missionary work in Peru. The Foreign Missions Board require that such a student spend a year in Scotland after training, getting pastoral experience with a local congregation.

The Foreign Missions Board decided in spring 1997 to approve Rosskeen as David's sponsor congregation, and in the summer of that year, he and his Peruvian wife Martha, with their boys John and Samuel, settled in Rosskeen for just over a year.

From their arrival, David and Martha gave their all. They set about getting to know everyone, and their home at Saltburn saw visitors on a frequent basis – Sunday dinners, weekday lunches and evenings together. Martha was unfazed at catering for numbers – she would just provide giant pavlovas! She enjoyed introducing us to Peruvian food, and was amazed at our bland tastes!

Martha is wholehearted and enthusiastic in all she does. She threw herself into the Mums and Toddlers group, being described by one mum as 'a ray of sunshine'. She would burst through the door with her arms open wide and a smile from ear to ear: 'Hello everyone' she would laugh. Not content with just organising activities for the children, Martha soon had the mums making papier-mâché bowls and masks, thus giving us the benefit of her creativity and engaging us in a social and relaxing activity while the children played around us. Many of us were found doing our 'homework' until midnight on the night before Toddlers!

The year flew by so quickly, but even although they were here for such a short time, they really cared about the people of Rosskeen and the Lord's work here. They were always busy, always visiting and always caring.

David was loved and much respected for his many gifts. In the pulpit he spoke boldly. His sermons were relevant, thorough and challenging – often looking at situations from a new perspective. He had an eye for picking the ordinary detail from a Bible story which really brought it to life. He was not afraid to tackle contentious issues in the light of Biblical truths, and through the Holy Spirit delivered sermons with a powerful message for both the unbeliever and for the Christian.

Coming from a different culture, David and Martha were able to see things from a different perspective, and they certainly opened our eyes on some issues! Martha was unable to understand our Highland reserve, being such a warm and demonstrative person herself.

John and Samuel quickly settled in, almost without introductions, as young children do. They were very popular with the Rosskeen gang. Bright and lively by nature, they regularly provided Dad with food for thought which he used in his sermons. John is football crazy and soon was numbered as a County fan – indeed, when he was asked what he would like for a leaving present, a County strip was his immediate choice! Younger brother Samuel delighted us all at Mums and Toddlers with his lovely renditions of 'Jesus Loves Me' in Spanish.

We are so thankful to God for the times we shared with them.

## New Car Park
By the grace of God an increasing number of people were attending the church services, and a solution had to be found to the problem of parking space. People were having to park by the side of the minor road and with up to four rows on the grass,

across the road from the church, people had to access the back
rows from the main A9 – a dangerous exercise.

The Deacons Court planned and built a new car park, thanks
to the Lord's provision. The car park came into operation in the
summer of 1997. It is already full, although most of our cars can
be accommodated between the car park and the area around the
church.

### Prayer

Throughout Derek's ministry, he has been determined that prayer
would be central to all we are and all we do at Rosskeen. Indeed,
as we see the number of prayer meetings continuing to grow we
can think back to Kenny's prayer in 1991 ('My over-riding desire
for the Rosskeen Church is that there would be many more prayer
meetings throughout the congregation and that they would be
well-attended. Then the Lord would bless – then our church
would be full to over- flowing.'), and thank God that he has
begun to answer it. We look forward in faith to the day when our
church will indeed be 'full to overflowing.'

'I'm sure we would all describe Rosskeen Free Church in
different ways. My dream description is for it to be known as
"the praying congregation". Not just that we are private prayer
warriors, but that we pray as a family, as a team, as an army –
together. It is SO encouraging. More than that, it is essential.
Without this, we are nothing' (Derek Lamont, Newsletter Sept/
Oct '97).

An important prayer initiative began in 1997 with the Prayer
Cells – small groups meeting monthly in various houses to pray.
Initially the main focus was outreach. We were asking God to
show us his plan – what to do and how to do it. Also on the
agenda were the congregational issues of the day, and the wider
church. These informal meetings were and are well looked
forward to, for the social aspect as well as the prayer. There is
great peace found in getting together with others and laying all
plans, concerns, needs and requests before the Lord. To know

that the Almighty One, who spread out the heavens with his hands and set the stars in their positions, is concerned with all our daily thoughts and problems – not just that, but LOVES to hear our prayers, is a wonderful and amazing blessing in itself. Even more wonderful is the joy of answered prayer, especially so as our Great God so often chooses to answer our prayers so lavishly and abundantly. (You will only know answered prayer if you pray!)

Another blessing has been the Young Women's Prayer Meeting. Those who had babies and toddlers had not tended to be at the existing Ladies Prayer Meeting – begun by Reta MacDonald – for fear of disrupting this 'engine-room' of congregational life. However, the desire for prayer was still there and we wondered how we could get around the fact of having the children with us. We could not impose on others to run a creche – we are already so grateful to those who so kindly and sacrificially give up their time to run the crèches at the morning services and the Young Women's Bible Study. It seemed that to have the children in the same room as us while we prayed would be too disruptive.

However, as we saw each other socially at each other's houses for coffee on odd mornings, we would share our concerns, and would often end up with a time of prayer, while the children always (well, nearly always!) just played quite happily around us. Indeed, often they seemed to sense the presence of the Holy Spirit, and were unnaturally quiet – even listening to the prayers. On one lovely occasion, two small girls also added their prayers.

These occasions just seemed to happen at the Saltburn Manse, where Martha's 'Always-Ready-For-Prayer' attitude was a great influence. We began to meet, with the children in with us. It isn't always perfect peace, but there is always someone to keep an eye on a little one, to give Mum peace to pray.

Other Prayer Meetings include the Men's Prayer Meeting at 8pm on Saturday evenings, the main Prayer Meeting and Bible Study at 7.30pm on Wednesdays (open to all), and the Early

Morning Prayer Meeting at 6.30am on some Thursdays. Full details of all meetings are always given on the weekly intimation sheet which is handed out at the Sunday Services, and also on the bi-monthly newsletter.

### Isobel's Story

Isobel Thomas tells us how the Lord took her to Rosskeen.

'Writing down how I became a member of the Rosskeen Free Church was quite an interesting exercise. It all began some way back...

'It was a daily tradition in our household that Will (our son) as a young boy, would rush in through the back door after school, and before setting eyes on me would shout out "Guess what, Mum?" This particular afternoon the "Guess what, Mum?" was "Our minister wears shocking pink socks!" The minister in question was Kenny MacDonald, the year was 1986, and my curiosity was awakened.

'By 1987 I was teaching at Park School, Invergordon and there regularly listened to the minister in pink socks as he spoke to the children at Assembly. I was soon aware that the sincerity and vitality of Kenny's love for his Lord outshone even shocking pink.

'At that time I was attending a local church, but something was amiss. I wasn't particularly connected up to my Lord, whom I had accepted as my Saviour many moons ago, as a young girl south of the Border.

'Since that time, I have taught in various local primary schools, where both Kenny (during his ministry) and Derek have been part of the ministry team. I have observed their witness for Jesus regularly and have been touched by it.

'I was pretty certain by this time that Rosskeen Free Church would have something for me, but still I backed off. You see, coming from the South, I didn't know the traditions of the Highlands or the history of the churches. Perhaps the Free Church was very strict. Perhaps the services were in Gaelic. All excuses,

I know, but they were very real, and there was a great anxiety about going to a new church on my own.

'In the end, the calling was too strong even for me, so I planned a visit to a church service with my class from Obsdale in July 1997, to see what it was like. What a warm welcome we were given!

'And that's how it all began. That's how the Lord helped me to come to Rosskeen. I have thanked him every day since and patiently await his timing to touch others in my family to join me at the church on the hill.' (Isobel Thomas)

## Ardross Games Night

In Rev John MacKay's time, Simon and Dorothy Allison had begun to hold Games Nights for the youth of Ardross on Friday evenings. Tragically Simon, who was a much loved elder, died after an illness in 1991. Dorothy continued with the Games Nights until she left the area in 1996. Les MacKay, a PE teacher Alness Academy, who had been a leader since moving to Ard in 1991, then took over the running.

The Games Nights were on most Fridays of the school in the Ardross Hall. Usually between ten and twenty kids came along, mostly from secondary school. In the winter months the hall was used for a variety of indoor team games and in the lighter nights the most popular choice was a game of football outside. Although the young folk did not attend the church, they listened to a 10-15 minute talk or discussion each week.

In 1998, Les took a well-earned break, and the Ardross Games Nights came to an end. Many youngsters benefited from the activities, sports and gospel message, and it is our hope that the seeds sown in their hearts will bear fruit to God's glory. We are very thankful to Les for his commitment to the event, and for his willingness to sacrifice his time for God's sake and his kingdom

**Youth Fellowship**

The Youth Fellowship has been going on since John and Mary MacKay opened their home to the teenagers of the church back in the early eighties. As the years have gone by, it has been great to see the numbers rise, and so many young people attending. It has also become a place for them to bring friends who don't go to church.

The YF meets every Sunday evening, after the service, in the Rosskeen Manse, and occasionally invades the homes of unsuspecting guest hosts. The age group varies from first year in the Academy upwards, with one or two very old 'youths' at the top of the range.

Past leaders of the Youth Fellowship have been David and Catriona Campbell and Malcolm and Kathryn MacLeod. Currently, Youth Worker Ricky leads the group in a regular programme of lively discussions, sometimes with guest speakers. Other activities in the syllabus may include a panel evening, a quiz, a video or somebody giving their testimony.

Rosskeen YF have no doubts about the relevance of the church to young people.:

'It was at a Free Church Camp that I was converted. There was a great atmosphere, and that's where I learned about Jesus. The church is very important to young people: there are so many things happening today, people can't handle it – they're just breaking up. The church gives me hope in something that I can't see in other people. The church is often put down today for being a dull and negative thing, but I think it's brilliant. I really look forward to church on Sundays because its such a friendly thing. I just can't get over how much love there is in the church' (Ruth MacNair).

'My friend invited me along. I think it's a better way of coping with life instead of going to drink and drugs' (Julie Carr).

'People think that to be a Christian there's got to be a bright light, but sometimes it's a gradual process. You've got to keep coming to church and strengthening what you believe' (Gary Gunn).

## The '20 Somethings'

The '20 Somethings' met for the first time on the 15th March 1998. The purpose of the group is to provide something for those who are too old to go to the Youth Fellowship and too young to go home and put their slippers on.

Since its beginnings, the meeting has been attended by varying age groups, and you don't actually have to be in your twenties to go along!

It provides a great opportunity to meet together in an informal environment, to blether, discuss Christian issues and enjoy the host's food! It's a great way to round off a Sunday.

## Mrs MacKenzie

At the AGM on Wednesday 18th March 1998, Mrs Dolly MacKenzie made known her intention to retire from teaching in the Sunday School after an amazing service of forty-two years. We are eternally indebted to Mrs MacKenzie for her enthusiastic, loyal and expert devotion to teaching the children.

The following is what she asked to be read out on her last Sunday as teacher – the Prizegiving Service in June.

'I must begin by setting the record straight. I have indeed been a Sunday School teacher for forty-two years. The first six of these were worked in Glasgow, and the remaining 36 years here, in Rosskeen.

'I know that it is a very great privilege to teach Bible Knowledge to children and young people. I know that the hope of Sunday School teachers is that these young people will have a foundation which cannot be shaken, on which to build their lives.

'I have felt privileged, too, to have handled so many pleasant, attractive young people during their years in Sunday School, before setting out on their adult lives.

'Down the years I have worked with Christian colleagues whom I warmly remember, and from whose walk and conversation I learned much. At present there are many who work for the church out of the public gaze, and whose efforts make me feel very small!

'Today ends a way of life for me. It used to be a question of looking over the lesson; praying about it; thinking hard about it; looking up reference books and hoping, when the time came, to acquit myself well.

'And now, I would pray for God's blessing on those who continue the work. And for Rosskeen Free Church Sabbath School I pray that God would enlarge its borders, bless those who teach in it, and bless and guide the children who learn in it, throughout their lives.

'Thank you all.

Mrs Dolly MacKenzie'

### Sunday School

We asked some teachers and pupils to share their memories and thoughts of Sunday School with us – some recent, and some not so recent!

'Is it really ten years since taking over from Anne Wilkie? I can still remember the first time I sat in on her class. Anne was so calm and had such a nice way with the little ones. When it finished I thought, "Lord, I'll never be able to do that!" The answer? His Word said to me, "I have chosen the foolish things of the world to confound the wise." What an encouragement, no excuses now and with his grace I'm glad to say, "Yes, ten great years."

'The numbers vary from year to year, between six and seventeen latterly, at which point it was decided to split the class and have another teacher. This was a great relief as most of the time was spent on numerous trips to the loo!! Today the average number in my class is ten to twelve.

'There have been so many special moments over the years, (why didn't I keep a diary?), anyway here are a few. Names have been withheld.

'On asking questions about the lesson – up go the hands – "Oh I think to myself, this is great, they have been listening, only to hear, "Cathy, I went swimming yesterday!" or "I'm going to my Gran's for dinner!"

'The little one who on hearing about Abraham and Isaac and how God provided another sacrifice said, "Poor Lamb". Then I remembered, "Behold, the Lamb of God, who taketh away the sin of the world." Who is teaching whom?

'The quietest they are is when they hear of Jesus before Pilate and carrying his own cross to be crucified. Then it is marvellous to tell them that he didn't stay dead, but that he is alive for evermore.

'They are so open and trusting. I am aware of the great responsibility I have as I open my mouth, and I count it a great privilege and joy to be part of this work. What was it Jesus said? "Except you be converted and become as little children ye shall not enter into the Kingdom of heaven.' (Mrs Cathy Dunlop, Teacher of Nursery Class)

'Since we were five years old we have gone to Sunday School, and have enjoyed it very much (apart from the learning work which we know is good for us but seems to be so hard to do!)

'Over the years we've been taught well and know that this will help us through life. Even at their ages, Dad and Mum can remember things from their Sunday School and we hope that we'll do the same.

'The work sheets in the Bible Class can be difficult but they make you think, and do help. The numbers have increased since we started and it's good that we even have to use the kitchen for a classroom.

'It's nice all the classes are together at the beginning of the services before we go to the Sunday School and what is even nicer is that we get a sweetie before we sit down!

'All in all, Sunday School is a great place to be and we know that it will help us later on in life' (Linda and Elaine MacIver).


'We both began Sunday School in the upper vestry with Mrs Anne Wilkie, who wore a brown woollen hat and carried a very small Bible. She used a green board and felt "stick pictures" to illustrate her stories. Once Richard was asked the names of Noah's three sons. His answer? Shem, Ham and Jaffa cakes! (Nothing to do with his favourite biscuits!)

'At one time we were moved to the top landing and Mrs Wilkie sat on a plastic chair at what seemed to be the edge of the stairs. We were always afraid she was going to fall down. If you really wanted to be daring then you sat at the banister and could look right down to the bottom of the stairs – SCARY!!

'We were both around at various times while the hall was being built. Under the vinyl in the gents toilet (or around that area) are the names of the people who helped to lay the foundation, engraved in the concrete.

'We have fond memories of Exam Time in the old Boiler Room. Five tables were set out, but the one in the alcove was greatly prized and sought after by everyone. The exam began at 10am, and at 11 o'clock precisely Mrs Mackenzie, Davie MacLeod and Lindsay MacCallum would have coffee and shortbread.

'Even if you didn't like coffee, you seemed to love the smell!

'James Campbell took a Psalmody Class. To begin with it was also held in the Boiler Room. When the numbers dropped to three (Richard, 'wee Mhairi" and Malcolm Campbell), it was held in James' house, and James took the exam.

'When there were more than three, the classes were held in the Alness Hall and Dr MacAulay used to come and hear the young folk at Exam time.

'Richard did Psalmody from 1983 to 1990 and Kevin from 1984 to 1989.

'James began a Bible Class at 11am on a Sunday morning. We can remember Duncan and Eilidh MacInnes attending, also Paula Jenkins and Christopher Robertson. After the Bible Class we had a cup of tea/juice, then we went into church to wait for Sunday School' (Richard and Kevin Stirling).

'At church we shake hands with a man at the door – he's there to make people feel welcome. When I was a wee boy, a man called Davie MacLeod used to shake my hand when I was going out of church. I prefer to go in the back door though, because there's always a queue to shake hands.

'I sit with the Sunday School at the front of the church, we bring money and give it to Mrs MacKenzie. She gives it to the minister. She gives you a sweet – I put it in my pocket and eat it after Sunday School.

'When the precentor starts singing, we sing out of our psalm books. I don't know the tunes but I do the best I can. I prefer singing with the Sunday School (the grown ups mumble a bit). Then the minister says a prayer and we stand and shut our eyes. Sometimes people whisper, and when we get to Sunday School our teacher gives us a telling off. The minister gives intimations about what things are happening, like Bible Studies, and then the precentor starts singing another psalm, and the Sunday School goes out to their classes.

'We have to learn a verse. It's nerve wracking saying a long one or a catechism. You've got to say it in front of the whole class and it's difficult if the others have said it really well. The teacher doesn't give rows if we can't say it. She just writes down what we've got to learn for next week on a card and gives us a v.g, good, quite good or a tick.

'My classroom is in the hall and sometimes in the kitchen if there's less than five. I can hear what's going on in other classes and sometimes we're disturbed by people going to the toilet.

'Our minister is Derek Lamont. Sometimes he comes to our school assembly, and I feel very proud when I see him at school.

'My teacher liked our old minister Kenny MacDonald's purple shoes' (Hugh Ferrier).

'At Sunday School, my friend and I sometimes talk. One day my mum was in the gallery and she could see us and she gave me a row afterwards.

'We sing psalms – sometimes I forget my Bible and I just try to sing along with everyone else.

'Our class meets in the middle of the hall. My teacher is Mrs MacInnes. I had Mrs Dunlop when I was younger. We have a story first and then we draw a picture. Sometimes people whine about what they've got to do. I like drawing best.

'A long time ago there were seventeen people in my class so we had to split up into two groups. Sometimes when there's too many of us we have to sit on the floor. People talk a lot at that time.

'I wear a shirt on Sundays and sometimes a tie too. I don't wear ties so much now because no-one else at Sunday School wears them – and they're too tight.

'Sometimes a service feels long, especially if it's hot. Sometimes I read my favourite Bible stories in church. When I was wee I kept my eyes open during the prayer and I would see some grown-ups smiling at me.

'At the Welfare of Youth Exam I was very nervous. We had to sit in the upper vestry where it was quite cold. We had to use a pen. Some of the questions were difficult especially when you had to remember verses, but mostly it was like a big workbook. I had to use a pen and we weren't allowed to speak. There were two of us doing the exam.

'At the end of Sunday School we wait at the church door for mummy and daddy.

'Sometimes someone gets baptised. When my sister was baptised I didn't know when to open my eyes, so I missed it all. My brother couldn't see what was happening because someone was standing in his way. I felt sad about not seeing her being baptised. I still don't know when to open my eyes or shut them because there are so many prayers at baptisms.

'The minister's job is to spread the good news about Jesus' (David Ferrier).

'Currently we have three classes in the Hall. If need be, the hall can be partitioned off for six classes. Our hall has become a much used and very useful church building. The other two classes meet in the upper vestry and the old boiler room.

'We who work in the Sunday School are not unmindful of the vital importance of what we try to do, or of the commendation in the Bible about knowing the Scriptures from a child upwards, and of how such knowledge can make us "wise unto salvation." We are aware of the first verse in Ecclesiastes, Chapter 12, and while in a small measure we may be "labourers sent forth to the harvest", we know that another said, "Paul planteth and Apollos watereth, but God giveth the increase."

'I write here the names of those who helped with Sunday School work since 1962, during those years when I taught in the Sunday School myself. If there is anyone whose name has been omitted from the list, I humbly apologise: Rev J. Muirden, Jenny Peterkin, Anne Muirden, Lilian MacKay (MacLennan), Anne-Marie Wallis (MacKenzie), Lindsay MacCallum, Katie Ross, Chrissie MacAulay, Anne Wilkie, Betty Dallas, Moira Bauld, Helen Sutherland, Ishbel Rodger, Kirsty MacInnes, Cathy Dunlop, Anne Ferrier, Aileen MacKay, Betty MacNair, Anne Campbell , Margaret Campbell.

'When needed Mrs Tom Cowie, Joyce Kirkwood and Janice MacLellan came in to help' (Mrs Mackenzie, Sunday School Superintendent).

**Derek**
The latter part of 1997 and first few months of 1998 saw Derek preaching away from Rosskeen quite a lot, including lecturing in Serbia.

'One very valuable lesson I have learned in all these engagements "away from home", is how much I love the congregation and how assured I am that this is where the Lord would have me work. In my case, absence definitely makes the heart grow fonder!

'My heart is in Rosskeen. My fervent prayer is that we can continue to work together as a team, and deepen our love and commitment to the Lord and each other. We must continue to work at the unity we have enjoyed, because it is an evidence of the Holy Spirit at work. More than that, we must improve on it, because in this area, as in all other areas, we fall short of the mark' (Derek, Newsletter May/June 1998).

## David's Story

'When I was first asked for my testimony, my initial reaction was, "OK, but why me?" I really wasn't sure I had much to say that would really interest people. I mean I haven't led a particularly remarkable life. I'm not famous, I've never been in prison, I didn't live a particularly "bad" life before becoming a Christian, and I certainly don't come from an abusive home. By today's standards I've had it pretty easy really. On reflection though, perhaps this was why my testimony might have some meaning to someone – an everyday and unremarkable life, touched by God.

'I was born some time ago in a small Borders town, but my family moved up to the Highlands when I was very young, and I consider it my home. I was certainly given a moral upbringing, although not necessarily Christian. I always believed in the existence of God, but never really saw it as all that big a thing in terms of "Real Life." Up to the age of about twelve or so I attended the Episcopalian church with my mother on more or less a regular basis. I was even confirmed, but I regret to say it meant very little to me. Eventually, I became very disillusioned with the whole thing and just stopped going. And that was more or less that, although I never really forgot about God, and far more importantly, he never forgot about me.

'At the age of seventeen I left school, packed my bags and went away to Aberdeen to study. By that stage in my life I had begun to get a little cynical, I knew there should be more to life – even an easy one like mine – but was beginning to despair of ever finding it. An old school friend invited me to go to church with herself and a cousin one Sunday, and I agreed, not expecting anything particularly impressive. Boy, was I wrong! The church in question was Bon Accord Free, and for the first time in my life I really heard the gospel preached. (This is not to say it had never been preached to me before, just that I'd never really heard it.) The people were another surprise. I'd been brought up with the image of the Free Kirk as being dour and dismal, but on the contrary they were friendly and welcoming. It certainly gave me food for thought. I went along a couple of times, but was still somewhat uncertain.

'Around that time a couple of very big changes occurred in my life. I failed an exam and was forced to drop out of college. Also I began a relationship with a girl from a Christian family, a relationship which went on to have a big influence on me. After we had been going out for a few months, she herself was converted. Strange as it may seem, even though I knew it would probably spell the end of our relationship, I was really pleased. But I still didn't consider it for myself.

'I returned to Aberdeen and stayed there for about a year and a half, getting by on a series of low paid, dead-end jobs, waiting for something to happen. I attended Bon Accord on and off, but made an effort not to let anyone get too close and never really mixed. The message, however, drew me back again and again. During that time I did split up with my girlfriend. I began spending as much time out as possible and generally slid deeper into the world every day. Eventually I lost my flat after an argument with my flatmate, and then my job too. I decided enough was enough, it was time to come home.

'I did some serious thinking about my life, and at the same

time started coming to Rosskeen regularly, twice every Sunday. At last I seemed to know what I was looking for, and I had an idea where to find it. Every week it seemed that the preaching was speaking to me and more of my questions were answered. But I still wasn't sure. After about three months, the June Communions rolled around and people began asking me serious questions. "Not yet," I said. Right up till the Thursday night, I discussed the issues with several people, and still I wasn't sure, I wasn't ready. That night I heard the Word of God, and the preacher spoke to me. I became aware that there might not be a next time, Christ wanted me now, as I was. I had no choice, how could I walk away? That had to be one of the scariest and most wonderful moments of my life. Suddenly a lot of what had happened over the last few years made sense and I saw everything in a new light.

'Of course, that was only the beginning. It hasn't always been easy, but God has been good to me. I've made many new friends, and seen a lot converted. I've had answered prayers and been led down roads I never expected to walk. I have no idea what the future holds, but one thing I know, as long as it holds God, I'll be all right' (David Ferguson).

## MacPhersons' Farewell

David, Martha, John and Samuel left for Moyobamba, Peru (Martha's home town) in September 1998. David's work is to set up a Bible College to train pastors. Martha will be assisting him with the administration. Newsletters are sent to Rosskeen and we give thanks to God that all is going well. We all love and miss them very, very much.

'A large congregation; stirring, challenging preaching; warm, sincere speeches and united fellowship over a sumptuous tea, undoubtedly sum up our farewell to the MacPhersons.

'Farewells traditionally stir the emotions of even the most stoical amongst us, and Friday 28th August proved to be a night of high emotion, especially when we learned that Martha was unable to join us for the occasion. The large gathering was stirred by the challenging message from David's father, the Rev John MacPherson. Both father and son have been blessed with the gift of a powerful, teaching ministry which we have been greatly privileged to enjoy. Following Mr MacPherson's address our gratitude for a year of rich spiritual blessings was warmly expressed through Rev Hugh MacCallum.

'In expressing thanks, David succumbed to the emotion which we all felt. Farewells are never easy and especially when they follow a year of blessed fellowship together. We certainly miss David's winsome preaching, Martha's smiling face and warm embrace, and John and Samuel's endearing ways. We feel sad but are also assured that they are answering the Lord's call. May they truly know his blessing and his grace as they do his work in Peru' (Kathleen MacIver, Sept/Oct '98 Newsletter).

### The Assistantship
At the congregational meeting on Wednesday 26th August, 1998, the congregation voted unanimously to call Iain MacLeay to be Rosskeen's first assistant minister with pastoral responsibilities.

Not only is it good to have these unsettled times decided by an appointment, but to know that the Holy Spirit is guiding our hearts and blessing us with unity is a tremendous encouragement and a source of great hope and excitement for the gathering in of Christ's Kingdom in this area.

### From Mull to Invergordon
'There must be a song in there somewhere! As 1998 progressed and I began to feel a real improvement in my health I started to wonder if there was life after depression. Could I get back into the Christian ministry? Would I be able to cope? Would anyone want me? These were real questions. As Isobel and I talked over them and began to long for a door to open, we just couldn't see that it would happen. The children were very happy in Mull – maybe we should just content ourselves, maybe in spite of all our longings

it just had to be fishing for prawns and not people!

'Then one night, when most sensible people should have been in bed, the phone rang! Hi, Derek here. How's things? To put it simply, that one phone call eventually led to the call from you as a congregation which I willingly and very happily accepted.

'Obviously there was much that happened in between those two calls, but here we are and we are truly thankful to God and the congregation of Rosskeen for this opportunity to serve him and to serve you as his servant.

'We have felt a very warm welcome from you as a congregation and have enjoyed worshipping with you. I have to say that in preaching and studying I have enjoyed a sense of God's presence which I haven't experienced in a long time and often wondered if I ever would. May God protect us from anything that would spoil the unity of this congregation or hinder the blessing of God that we long for and look for.

'There has been a lot of hustle and bustle around the Nurseries over these past weeks. To all those who have helped in any way we say a very big THANK YOU. The new shower and kitchen are just superb. Please, if you are passing, feel free to call. We would love to see you and I'm sure you would be encouraged by what has been done in the house.

'Irene, Alison and Douglas are enjoying being part of the congregation but they really do miss their friends in Mull. This move and the uncertainty of these past few years has been very difficult for them and for my long suffering wife. We would really appreciate your prayers that as a family we would know God's blessing and his help in all the adjustments that need to be made in each of our lives.

'It is good to be with you.

'Iain MacLeay.'


We are indeed a truly privileged people to have been blessed with the ministers God has given us – past and present.

**Congregational Treasurer**

As Rosskeen Free Church has increased in size over recent years, the increase in givings has meant that, through church legislation, we have been entitled to call an assistant minister. This both eases the workload and generates more!

One man who has tirelessly and unassumingly coped with a vastly increased workload is Mr Roy Harman, our Treasurer.

As the congregation has grown, there has been the need to provide sound book-keeping regarding outreach, maintenance of buildings, Assistantships and Youth Workers. This, coupled with new and stringent accounting practices demanded by the law of the land, has made Roy's job very time consuming.

He serves the Lord in this area and had done for many years and under several ministries, with a meticulous dignity and good order. He never complains and has been known to smile broadly when gaining or saving a few pence in the Lord's Treasury!

We continue to be very dependent on his skills and thank God for his dedication and service in this practical field.

**New Elders and Deacons**

In March 1999 Mr Wildon Campbell, Mr Derek Hannan and Mr Davy Maclellan were added to the Eldership, and Mr Donald Gordon, Mr Hamish MacDonald and Mr Donald MacIver were added to the Deaconate.

**'Campaigners 4'**

A number of children from Alness and Milnafua continually reminded Catriona that there was no Campaigners Group in their neck of the woods. In April of 1999, Alness Campaigners got under way, being held in the Perrins Centre. Catriona Lamont, Ricky MacDonald and Avril MacLennan are the leaders of the group, which meets on Thursdays.

## Colombian Connection

It was David MacPherson who suggested that we, as a congregation, help to support Manuel and Patti Reãno, and their children Catalina, Cristina and Benjamin. Manuel is a lecturer at the Bible Seminary in Colombia, having completed his theology course at the Free Church College (hence the connection with David). The congregation had the privilege of hearing him preach before the family left Scotland to take up his new and very challenging appointment. The Seminary is the biggest non-denominational seminary in Colombia, and the Reãnos are working in the country under the auspices of an organisation called Latin Link. Manuel also has a heavy schedule of preaching engagements in different churches, with expository, Scripture-centred preaching being much in demand, and he has been invited to train lay preachers in two churches.

The Free Church of Scotland is one of the Reanos supporters. David proposed that Rosskeen make a further commitment to the missionary family, and the Deacons Court agreed to support them for a period of five years. Such support allows the congregation to have a focus of missionary interest in South America, with the Reãnos, the MacPhersons and also Angus and Anita Lamont in Peru. It is always great to read their latest E-mail, and our prayers for the Lord's blessing upon these families are very much at the heart of our worship in Rosskeen today.

At Communion time, there is an opportunity for people to publicly profess their faith in the Lord Jesus Christ for the first time.

### Anne's Story

We draw to a close with a testimony from one of our newest Christians:

'Come unto me, all ye that labour and are heavy laden, and I will give you rest. Take my yoke upon you, and learn from me; for I am meek and lowly in heart: and ye shall find rest upon your souls. For my yoke is easy, and my burden is light' (Matt. 11:28-30).

'Where do you find this in the Bible, when you haven't been brought up in the 'church', and when Bible reading was never part of your life?

'This was the reality for me – until my neighbour asked me to go to church with her. My life was never to be the same again. Little did I know that God had drawn me to Rosskeen to show me the burdens I carried in my life. He wanted me to give them to him.

'Up until that point I had never really given God much thought. I was weighed down with the everyday worries of a busy family life. I suffered extreme migraine headaches and was always tired and didn't really have time for anyone else.

'For the first time in my life I started to pray. I brought my worries to God and he dealt with them one by one. He was so patient with me. I learned that he listened to me. Now, for me PRAYER is the vital backbone of my Christian walk. I soon found my way to the Wednesday Prayer Meeting. It was a joy to share with God's people as I became part of the Church Family.

'As for finding my way round the Bible –

'I discovered that reading God's Word daily and seeing how he wants me to live my life has opened up a new world to me.

'I have never suffered a migraine headache since giving my burdens to Jesus. Now I have time to listen to others, and I love to tell them that what Jesus has done for me, he can do for them!' (Anne Simpson).

# CHAPTER 8

# TIMES CHANGE

Time is indeed a strange commodity when we stop to contemplate it. In our busy lifestyles, days and weeks fly by at an alarming rate, seeming to gather pace as the years go by. And yet, events which happened long ago can sometime seem so close. Our memories are close to our hearts, whether painful or delightful.

What does he who was there 'In the beginning ...' think of the lives we are living today? He who knows the end from the beginning; he to whom a thousand years are as the blink of an eye; he who sees the whole picture of human history, with the Cross of Calvary as its pivotal and defining moment?Do we take time to think of him in our daily business?

And what of Eternity – how can our earthly centred minds grasp the reality of Eternity? We pay so much attention to the health and well-being of our bodies, but what care do we take of our souls, which, being eternal, are infinitely more valuable than our bodies? Reader, what provision have you made for your soul's eternal rest? Have you taken the time to consider his words: 'I am The Way, The Truth and The Life. No one comes to the Father except through me' (John 14:6). Have you pondered what the Cross was all about? Have you seen the beauty and the wonder of the love of God in that ugly and shocking event, as he, in human form, died in our place?

The passing of time over the last 100 years was poignantly illustrated at Rosskeen's annual Sunday School Picnic on Saturday, 12th June 1999.

Two double decker buses drove from one end of the parish to the other, gathering up excited Campaigners and Sunday School children, together with the braver members of the congregation (the others followed by car! )

Streamers flew from the windows, Iain MacLeay would not stop swinging from the holding rails, and the children were on their 126th lively rendition of "When Zion's Fortunes ..." as the buses arrived at Rosemarkie beach. Children were in the water in the blink of an eye, leaving a wake of assorted clothing strewn across the beach behind them. Those unprepared for swimming went in anyway and later were to be found shivering under over-sized fleeces donated by kindly onlookers. Undeterred by the fine misty drizzle, the afternoon was enjoyed in time-honoured fashion: the ice-cream moustaches, the blue lips, the soggy towels, the balls of sandy socks, the lost jumper; the smiles, the laughter, the greetings of good friends, the old and the young; the banter of the tug-of-war (Alness v. Invergordon) and the cheating of the races; the much needed cups of steaming tea, and the tables piled high with sandwiches and the endless delicious baking.

Sitting on benches enjoying the scenes, were Mrs Ena MacIver, aged 85 (contributor to Chapter 2) watching some of her twenty-nine grandchildren; Mrs Anna MacLeod, aged 89, with her great grand-daughter, Isla; and Mr. And Mrs. Roy and Katie Harmon, who have been in Rosskeen since 1953.

What were their thoughts on the pictures in front of them? How many Sunday School picnics had they enjoyed? What memories had they of their children growing up – running and laughing and enjoying the very same activities, right down to the 'baggies' on the bus home? What memories of the camaraderie of running the races themselves as young people? What memories of the passing years, and of how the Almighty has dealt so kindly and gently with his people?

Times change, and in a Highland church during a century of momentous social change, many things have changed considerably. Some things, however, do not change, and we must all consider where we stand in relation to the claims of Jesus Christ. One day, we shall answer for our decision, 'For we must all appear before the judgement seat of Christ' (2 Cor. 5:10).

'The grass withers and the flowers fall, but the word of our God stands forever' (Isaiah 40:8).

'As a father has compassion on his children,
   so the LORD has compassion on those who fear him;
for he knows how we are formed,
   he remembers that we are dust.
As for man, his days are like grass,
   he flourishes like a flower of the field;
the wind blows over it and it is gone,
   and its place remembers it no more.
But from everlasting to everlasting
   the LORD's love is with those who fear him,
   and his righteousness with their children's children –
with those who obey his covenant
   and remember to obey his precepts.
The LORD has established his throne in heaven,
and his kingdom rules overall' (Psalm 103:13-19).


JESUS CHRIST IS THE SAME YESTERDAY
AND TODAY AND FOREVER (Hebrews 13:8).

# Index

Acharacle 41

Achnagarron 33. 79, 103

Achnagarron Church 104, 105

Achnagarron – pipe tune 33

Achnagarron Smithy 12

Afternoon Fellowship 75, 101-3, 139

Aird, Gustavus 9

Aird, John 25

Allison, Alex 34

Allison, Christie 35

Allison, Dorothy 163

Allison, Simon 87, 102, 163

Alness 22, 23, 26, 28, 31, 34, 42, 45, 46, 49, 52, 53, 54, 56, 63, 64, 65, 77, 79, 81, 82, 86, 87, 91, 102, 104, 116, 117, 130, 133, 135, 136, 154, 163, 168, 177

Alness Baptist Church 136

Alness Parish Church   35

Alness West School 23

Anderson, Bessie 102

Ardnamurchan 59, 77

Ardross 16, 17, 23, 26, 36, 45, 50, 54, 55, 62, 71, 117, 126, 128, 163

Ardross Castle 23, 129

Ardross Church 24, 34-5, 63, 126, 129, 131

Ardross Church Trust Deed 127-8

Ardross – psalm tune 33

Armstrong, Claire 117

Auchentoul 11

Bain, Alex 54

Bain, Mrs 54

Baptism 31, 47, 71

Barbaraville 69

Bauld, Moira 171

Beaton, Rev Archibald 14

Bell, Mrs 22

Belleport 12

Bell ringers 38-9

Bible Class 64, 169

Black, Dr. I. I. 13

Black, Ian 76

Black, Mary 76

Black, Pamella 74, 130

Black, Patricia (Trisha) 74, 130-2

Blythswood 115

Boag, Thomas 53

Boath School 35

Boyd, Fiona 117

Bridgend School 23, 59, 61, 64, 77, 86

Bruce, Donnie 47, 49, 55, 61, 62

Bruce, John 66

Burn, The 116

Cameron, Alex 17

Cameron, Roddie 38, 47

Cameron, Ronnie 47

Cameron, Stuart 47

Cameron, Rev Prin W C 62

Campaigners 101, 154-6, 177, 180

Campbell, Anne 59, 171

Campbell, Catriona 164

Campbell, David 164

Campbell, James 78, 87, 88, 94, 102, 108, 109, 168, 169

Campbell, Malcolm 168

Campbell, Margaret 171

Campbell, Rev Norman 43

Campbell, Wildon 132, 154, 177

Caol 75

Careforce 156

Care Worker 112-4

Carment, Rev David 9, 43

Carr, Julie 164

Chalmers, Shirley 136

Christian Basics Bible Study 123

Church, Building the 11ff

Columbia 178

Communion 20, 32, 33, 36, 46, 48, 53, 62, 66, 70, 73, 75, 82, 84, 117, 121, 136, 140, 178

Cowie, Tom 99, 102, 171
Creich 20
Culcairn 24
Dallas, Betty 171
Dallas, Robertson 36
Dalmore 61, 107
Dalnevie 24
Deacons Court 80, 87, 102, 136
Delny 61, 69, 71
Denoon family 11-12
Dingwall 17, 43, 115
Dingwall Academy 42
Doorkeepers 38-9
Dress for church 30, 33, 47, 133-4
Dryden, George 35
Dryden, Mary 15, 25, 29, 30, 32
Dublin 35, 128
Duff, Uisdean 47
Dunlop, Cathy 98, 167, 170, 171
Evanton 23, 59
Family Camp 119
Family life 17-21, 29
Family worship 17-18, 49-50, 70
Fast days 30-31
Fearn Free Church 153
Fellowship meetings 96
Ferguson, David 172-4
Ferguson, Hugh 11
Ferintosh 116
Ferrier, Anne 85, 91, 136, 171
Ferrier, David 102, 171
Ferrier, Hugh 7, 78, 170
Ferrier, Hugh (Jr) 102
Ferrier, Mairi 102
Finance Committee 35, 38
Finlayson, Rev Prof R K 57
Fortrose Free Church 140
Fort William 67
Freewill Offering envelopes 36
Funerals 31
Gaelic 17, 19, 20, 22, 25, 33, 46
Gallie, Jessie 39

Glasgow 77
Gordon, Donald 177
Gordon, Duncan 140, 142
Graham, Rev C 57
Graham, Davie 36
Graham, John 99
Grahams of Strathy 35
Gulf War 112-3
Gunn, Catriona 117, 118
Gunn, Gary 136, 165
Gunn, Jimmy 101
Gunn, Lewis 136
Gunn, Mr 53
Gunn, Steve 136
Hall, New 103-10
Halkirk 20
Ham, Barbara 101
'Handers' family 32, 33
Hannan, Derek 177
Hannan, Dorothy 118
Harmon, Katie 47, 51, 181
Harmon, Roy 35, 47-8, 55, 62, 71, 88, 142, 177, 181
Harvest thanksgiving 30-31
Hebron School 72
Highways and Byways 55, 115-8
HMS Natal 39
Howe, Rev A 61, 62, 129
Hutcheson Fraser, Rev John 10
Inchindoun 45
India 72, 90, 97, 111, 138
Invergordon 25, 26, 42, 46, 50, 65, 85, 87, 101, 104, 107, 118, 154, 155, 162
Invergordon Academy 61, 78, 99
Invergordon Sunday School 98-100
Jehovah's Witnesses 78, 81
Jenkins, Paula 169
Jenkins, Taff 108, 109
Kennedy Cameron, Prof John 17
Kennedy, Dr 17
Kennedy, John 36, 55

Kilchoan 75
Kildary 104
Kildermorie 35
Kinlochbervie 20
Kilmuir Easter Free Church 66, 68, 69, 71
Kiltearn 75
Kirk Session 82, 95, 102, 126, 135
Kirkwood, Hugh 154
Kirkwood, Joyce 171
Knockbain Free Church 101
Ladies' Bible Study 86, 87
Ladies' Meeting 86
Ladies' Prayer Meeting 96, 97, 161
Laidler, Rev 35
Lairg Free Church 38
Lamont, Amy 102
Lamont, Angus 178
Lamont, Anita 178
Lamont, Anne 145
Lamont, Barbara 145
Lamont, Rev Calum 84, 86
Lamont, Catriona 112, 116, 123, 149-50, 151, 177
Lamont, Rev Derek 101, 102, 111, 116, 123, 135, 145-79
Lamont, Rev. Donald 145, 147
Lamont, Joan 145
Lamont, Joe 102
Lamont, Peter 145
Lamont, Scott 102
Leitch, Rev Duncan 43, 57, 59
Leprosy Mission 62
Lewis, Isle of 90
Library 135
Lipp, David 135, 146
Loanreach 34
Lochinver 20
Logie 71
Logie Easter 40
London 77, 90
MacAskill, Grant 151-2

MacAulay, Callum 62, 88, 168
MacAulay, Chrissie 86, 88, 171
MacAulay, Norman 64, 65
MacAulay, Rosemary 64
MacBean, Beana 13
MacCallum, Aeneas 59, 75
MacCallum, Flora 59, 74
MacCallum, Rev Hugh 39, 48, 59-76, 77, 81, 109, 175
MacCallum, Rev John 81
MacCallum, Kenny 76
MacCallum, Lindsay 62, 74, 81, 85, 96, 168, 171
MacCallum, Sandra 75
McDairmaid, Rev D 34
MacDonald, Ada 15
MacDonald, Alasdair 15, 38
MacDonald, Alison 72, 90-2, 97, 137, 139, 145
MacDonald, Angela 85
MacDonald, Father Bernard 61
MacDonald, Cathy 15
MacDonald, Debbie 145
MacDonald, Derek 93
MacDonald, Rev Donnie G 146
MacDonald, Ella 103
MacDonald, Hamish 152, 177
MacDonald, Isa 15, 22, 23
MacDonald, Jeannie 15
MacDonald, Jimmy 35, 39
MacDonald, Rev John 15-41, 53
MacDonald, Rev John (Kiltearn) 31, 44, 45
MacDonald, John (Jr) 15
MacDonald, Rev J A 57
MacDonald, Mrs John 15, 16, 21, 22, 31, 45
MacDonald, Rev Kenny 13, 45, 48, 75, 89, 90-144, 145, 147, 148, 160, 162, 170
MacDonald, Mary 15
Macdonald, Melissa 157

Macdonald, Rev. Neil 145, 146
MacDonald, Reta 13, 90-3, 95, 97,
    98, 108, 114, 123, 137, 138, 139,
    140, 142, 144, 145, 147, 148, 161
Macdonald, Ricky 156-8, 164, 177
MacDougall, Rev Archibald 59
MacGregor, Alastair 61
MacGregor, Donald 68
MacGregor family 61
MacGregor, Morag 68-71
MacGregor, R G 55
MacGregor, Rod 35, 61
MacGregor, Roy 68, 102
Macinnes, Duncan 169
Macinnes, Eilidh 169
Macinnes, Kirsty 170, 171
MacIntosh, Dan 35
MacIntosh, Joan 15, 16, 17, 21, 25,
    29, 30, 32, 33, 34
MacIntosh, Prof 20
MacIver, David 102
MacIver, Donald 61, 109, 177
MacIver, Elaine 102, 108, 168
MacIver, Ena 15, 22, 25, 30, 31, 33,
    45, 48, 181
MacIver family 48, 53, 80
MacIver, Hugh 48, 49,72-4, 80, 81,
    95, 96, 102, 154
MacIver, John 110
Maciver, Kathleen 175
MacIver, Kenny 80, 132, 135, 154
MacIver, Kenny (Sn) 31, 35, 47,
    48, 52, 55, 60-2, 66, 68, 80
MacIver, Linda 102, 108, 168
MacIver, Murdo 61, 85, 87, 109,
    110, 126, 154
MacIver, Peggy 80
MacIver, Richard 80
MacIver, Rory 102
MacIver, Rev S 43, 66
MacIver, Sheana 47
MacKay, Aileen 88, 171

MacKay Bequest 36
MacKay, Donald 23
MacKay, Ellen 36
MacKay, Georgie 35
MacKay, Jean 15, 16, 29, 30, 31, 33-
    4, 36
MacKay, John (Jr) 86
Mackay, Rev John L 45, 48, 62, 77-
    89, 93, 96, 156, 163, 164
Mackay, Les 163
MacKay, Lillian 97, 99, 101, 171
Mackay, Mary 86, 164
MacKay, Mr (Schoolmaster) 32
MacKenzie, Alina 53
MacKenzie, Anne Marie 64, 65
MacKenzie, A G 12, 15, 23, 31, 33,
    36, 37, 38, 41
MacKenzie, Baby 47
MacKenzie, Colin 64, 74
MacKenzie, David 74
MacKenzie, Doddy 37
MacKenzie, Dolly 17, 50, 52-3, 56,
    66, 165-6, 168, 169, 171
MacKenzie, Elizabeth 100, 101
MacKenzie, Hugh 107, 109
MacKenzie, Jessie 74-6
MacKenzie, John 11, 35, 38, 64, 65
MacKenzie, John (Achnagarron) 35
MacKenzie, Johnny 33
MacKenzie, Major 11
MacKenzie, Margaret 59
MacKenzie, Marie 86, 87
MacKenzie, Mr (Achnagarron) 31
MacKenzie, Mr (Invergordon) 47
MacKenzie, Murdo 13
MacKenzie, Rory 36
MacKenzie, Sandy 37
MacKenzie, Willie 60, 76
MacKenzies of Strathy 35
MacKinnon, Catherine 47
MacKinnon, Granny 69
MacKinnon, Jock 115

MacLean, Neil 117
MacLean, Willie 35, 55
Macleay, Alison 176
Macleay, Douglas 176
MacLeay, Rev D 43
Macleay, Rev. Iain 175, 181
Macleay, Irene 176
Macleay, Isobel 175
MacLellan, Davy 120, 133-4, 154, 177
MacLellan, Janice 119-24, 171
McLennan, Mr and Mrs 27
Maclennan, Avril 177
MacLeod, Angus 107
Macleod, Anna 181
MacLeod, Davie 15, 24, 35, 39, 47, 49, 52-3, 55, 61-2, 68, 75, 81, 88, 93, 109, 133-5, 142, 168, 169
MacLeod, DJ 55
MacLeod, G 55
MacLeod, George 35, 66, 87
MacLeod, Helen 133
MacLeod, John 49
MacLeod, Rev John 73
MacLeod, John Murdo 55
MacLeod, Kathryn 136, 164
MacLeod, Rev K 61
MacLeod, Malcolm 101, 164
MacLeod, Marion 117, 136
MacLeod, Mhari 31, 50, 62
MacLeod, Mr (headmaster) 46
MacLeod, Mhari 49, 50, 62
MacLeod, Neil 46
MacLeod, W 55
MacLeod, Walter 15, 25, 29, 30, 32, 39, 133
MacMillan, Rev Neil and Mrs Louise 117
MacMillan, Mary 117
MacNair, Betty 171
MacNair, Ruth 164
MacPherson, David 158, 159, 174-5, 178

MacPherson, John 158, 159, 174-5
MacPherson, Rev. John 175
MacPherson, Martha 158, 159, 174-5
MacPherson, Samuel 158, 159, 174-5
MacRae, Rev Kenneth 54
Maggie the Mason 33
Manse 16, 63, 65
Manson, Mary 15, 22, 25, 29, 30, 32, 102
Marriages 31, 71
Maryburgh 42, 43
Matheson, Anne 59
Matheson, Rev. Farquhar 145
Matheson, Gary 154
Matheson, Myra 59
Membership 125
Men's Meetings 126, 162
Merry, Elizabeth 90, 138
Millcraig 24
Miller, Billy 109
Milnafua 78, 84, 85, 177
Milton 100, 153-4
Minibus 132
Mission 85 101, 111
Mission 92 115-8
Morison, Cailean 126
Morison, Christine 126, 154
Morison, Colin 126
Morison, Katie 126
Morison, Sam 126
Morrison, Margaret 136
Morrison, Rev Ronald 136
Mossfield 37
Mothers and Toddlers Group 117-8, 136, 158
Moultivie 27
Mounsey, Mr 61
Muirden, Anne 44, 45, 53, 56, 171
Muirden, Rev George and Mrs 42
Muirden, Rev John R 42-58, 62, 63, 66, 171

Munro, A 43
Munro, Catherine 66-67
Munro family 61
Munro, Helen 22
Munro, Katie 22
Munro, Minnie 27
Munro, Miss 32
Murchison, John 35, 49
Murchison, Mrs 43
Newsletter 114, 133, 135
Nigg 61, 93
Noble, Rev John 13
Novar 59
Nurseries, The 71
Oban 67
Obsdale School 143
Opening of present church 13
Orkney 90
Park Primary School 61, 162
Pastoral Team 114
Paterson, Ian 153
Perrins, C W Dyson 23, 35, 128, 129
Perrins, Mr 130
Perrins Road Hall 29, 31, 33, 79
Peterkin family 48
Peterkin, Jenny 15, 22, 30, 33, 39, 47, 50, 52, 171
Peterkin, Sollie 35, 45, 46, 55
Place, The 116, 117
Plenderleith, Margaret 72
Portmahomack 51
Prayer Meeting 32, 46, 47, 62, 75, 95, 115, 134, 162
Pre-1900 history 9-10
Raasay 20, 41
Rankin, Rev Roddy 93-6
Reãno, Benjamin 178
Reãno, Catalina 178
Reãno, Cristina 178
Reãno, Rev. Manuel 178
Reãno, Patti 178

Reid, Jessie 13
Reid, John 11, 32, 34
Reid, Mrs 39
Religious education in school 18
Renwick, Catriona 101
Renwick, Fachie 150
Renwick, Rev Farquhar 101, 115, 117
Renwick, Rhoda 117
Resolis 13, 145
Robertson, Christopher 169
Rodger, Ishbel 171
Rogart 20
Rosemarkie 51
Ross, Rev Alastair 23, 28, 39
Ross, Alex 39
Ross, Angus 70
Ross, Catherine 61
Ross, David 11
Ross, Rev Donald 57, 58, 66, 67, 68, 71
Ross, Donald 24, 32, 34, 39, 40, 41, 43, 47
Ross, D W 23, 35, 36, 39, 49
Ross family 32
Ross, John 11, 35
Ross, John (Jordan) 39
Ross, John (Seaforth) 36
Ross, John (Stoneyfield) 36
Ross, Rev John 10
Ross, Rev John (UF) 34
Ross, Katherine 70
Ross, Katy 66, 68, 171
Ross, Ken 39
Ross, Morag 61
Ross, Pete 35, 49
Ross, Mr (Glasgow House) 32, 33
Ross, Mrs 22, 25
Ross, Nigel 13
Ross, Simon 39
Ross, William 35, 39, 55
Rosses of Strathy 35

*Ross-shire Journal* 39, 42, 67
Sabbath observance 19-20, 29
Saltburn 112, 123, 149, 158, 161
Sandwick 51
Scotsman, The 91
Scott, Arthur 109
Scourie 20
Second World War 37-9, 129
Services 32
Session Clerk 93
Shorter Catechism 18, 21, 30, 49
Simpson, Anne 178-9
Skye, Isle of 90
Sloan, Rev R 61
Smart, Rev Chris 117
Smelter, Invergordon 93
Social Work 113
Sonamarg 90, 145
South Lodge 87, 98, 100, 101
St. Columba's Free Church 145
Stewart, Duncan 35
Stewart, Kenneth 36
Stewart, Miss 22, 23
Stewarts of Strathay 35
Stirling, David 118
Stirling, Donald 77, 8-5, 87, 96, 107, 126, 133, 135
Stirling, Janice 81, 83, 85, 96-7, 101-3, 126
Stirling, Jessie 84, 97
Stirling, Kevin 81, 154, 168, 169
Stirling, Mark 81
Stirling, Mhairi 118-9
Stirling, Michelle 118
Stirling, Nicole 118
Stirling, Richard 87, 154, 168, 169
Stirling, Scott 118
Stittenham 25
Stoneyfield 32
Strathpeffer 139

Strathpeffer Convention 53
Strathy 20, 35
Student Placement 150-2
Sunday School 19, 21-4, 34, 45, 47, 49-50, 52-3, 64-6, 73-4, 78, 84-5, 87, 104, 106-7, 118, 153-4, 157, 165-71, 180
Sutherland, Davine 50
Sutherland, Hansi 50
Sutherland, Helen 171
Sutherland, Hugh 35
Sutherland, Ross 50
Tain Academy 17
Tape ministry 87
Tarbat 42
Taylor, Opal 112-4
Thom, J E 129
Thomas, Isobel 162-3
Tuach, Willie 35
Urquhart, Hugh 32
Urqhuart, Mr 21, 25
Urquart, Mr and Mrs 32
Video Project 135
Wallis, Anne Marie 136, 171
Weager, Andy 101, 126
Welfare of Youth Exams 22, 52-4, 168, 170
Wilkie, Rev David and Mrs Anne 84-5, 96, 98-101, 167, 168, 171
Will, Sam 19
Wilson, Rosemary 65
Wishart, Ruth 91, 139
Winchester, Mrs 36
Womans Foreign Mission Association 36, 46
Young Women's Prayer Meeting 161
Youth Fellowship 86, 116, 131, 157, 164
Youth Worker 156-8

Christian Focus Publications publishes biblically-accurate books for adults and children. The books in the adult range are published in three imprints.

*Christian Heritage* contains classic writings from the past.

*Christian Focus* contains popular works including biographies, commentaries, doctrine, and Christian living.

*Mentor* focuses on books written at a level suitable for Bible College and seminary students, pastors, and others; the imprint includes commentaries, doctrinal studies, examination of current issues, and church history.

For a free catalogue of all our titles, please write to
Christian Focus Publications,
Geanies House, Fearn,
Ross-shire, IV20 1TW, Great Britain

For details of our titles visit us on our web site
http://www.christianfocus.com